"I read this book twice and I love the way it approaches everything, it shows the real importance of the places without losing sight of the focus, which is far beyond the places, the stones and sand, the dirt and antiquities. It keeps reminding pilgrims that what they came to see is an empty tomb, while the one they came to get to know better is a risen Lord. In that sense the author is not providing pilgrims with a tour guide as much as with a testimony, a witness to his own faith. May God reward him with his blessings. No doubt this new approach to pilgrimage and to holy places will help pilgrims to go more in-depth towards a spiritual experience through visiting the historical places. This work is a blessing for all those who will read it and take inspiration from the content and identify with the goal."

> – REV. ELIAS CHACOUR
> *President of Prophet Elias College in Galilee. Author of*
> Blood Brothers. *A Palestinian Christian promoter of*
> *reconciliation among the three faiths in the Holy Land.*

"The book is wonderful; more than wonderful! It will be required reading for all traveling with me to the Holy Land."

> – REV. CHARLES ANTEKEIER
> *Veteran Holy Land pilgrimage leader.*

"I can't say how much I enjoyed reading the manuscript. It is not just a guide-book to the Holy Land, but a treasure of spiritual insights into what the Holy Land means to so many people. The ecumenical approach is wonderful and I feel that not only Christians of all denominations will enjoy it but Muslims and Jews as well."

> – REV. JOSEPH GIRZONE
> *Author of the best-seller,* Joshua in the Holy Land, *and*
> *other books in the Joshua series.*

"... a wonderful mingling of history, bible, people and places, with an excellent presentation for a pilgrim to understand and experience the land and culture of Christ and his times, as well as of today...more than a tour book, it is a Key to opening a wonderful and prayerful experience."

> – AUXILIARY BISHOP NICHOLAS J. SAMRA
> *A leader of Palestinian Christians in the U.S.A.*

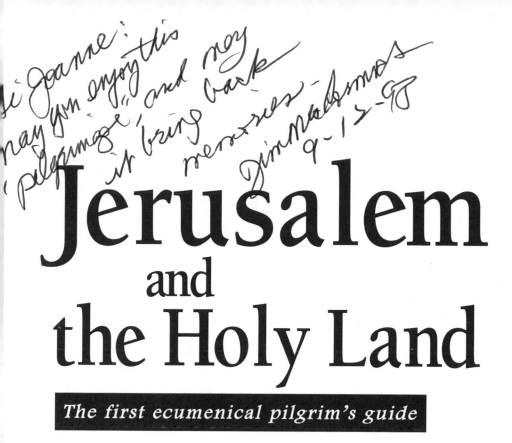

Hi Joanne:
May you enjoy this
"pilgrimage", and may
it bring back
memories —
Jim Mc Cormick
9-12-98

Jerusalem
and
the Holy Land

The first ecumenical pilgrim's guide

James R. McCormick

Rhodes & Easton

TRAVERSE CITY, MICHIGAN

Published by Rhodes &Easton
121 E. Front Street, 4th Floor, Traverse City, Michigan 49684

Publisher's Cataloging-in-Publication Data
McCormick, James R.
     Jerusalem and the Holy Land : the first ecumenical pilgrim's guide / James R.
     McCormick. – Traverse City, Mich. :
     Rhodes & Easton, 1997
        p.   ill.   cm.
     Includes bibliographical references and index.
     ISBN: 0-9649401-3-2
     1. Christianity–History. 2. Jerusalem–Description and travel.
     3. Holy Land–Description and travel. 4. Jerusalem–History. 5. Holy Land–
        History. I. Title.
DS109.M33 1997
915'.694–dc21 96-72180

PROJECT COORDINATED BY JENKINS GROUP, INC.

00   99   98   *   5   4   3   2   1

Printed in the United States of America

*This book is dedicated to the
achievement of a just peace among
the Christians, Jews and Muslims
of the Holy Land. When it happens
may it spread from there to
the rest of the world.*

*On a more personal level
I dedicate the book to the
primary pilgrims in my
life's journey: Marilyn
and our children Dan,
Ginny and David.*

CONTENTS

Part Four – Now, About Your Trip

ACKNOWLEDGMENTS

I wish to acknowledge the much appreciated support and encouragement of many people who aided the writing and editing of this book. First and foremost is my loving wife, Marilyn, for her unwavering confidence in my ability to accomplish this and her patience during my endless evenings of writing. Then there are the fellow pilgrims whose lively curiosity inspired me to undertake the rather daunting task. Grace Glynn's painstaking and cheerful typing of the original manuscript and the generous assistance of my secretary, Lorraine VenZuch, with a million details have not gone unnoticed.

Many gracious people have lent their time to critique the manuscript as to form and content, adding immeasurably to the final version, especially in its sensitivity to cultural and religious feelings, not to mention its historical accuracy. These include Mike Ready, Editorial Page Editor of the *Traverse City Record-Eagle;* Will Case-Daniels, world traveler; Rev. Charles Antekeier, long-time pilgrimage guide; Rev. Robert Wild, author of a wonderful book on Holy Land pilgrimage; Pat Dyson, veteran Holy Land tour guide; Dr. Gary Burge of Wheaton College Theology Department, author of a recent book on evangelical attitudes towards the Palestinian Christians; Rev. Gerald Micketti; Professor Glen

Bowman, noted anthropologist of pilgrimage, University of Kent at Canterbury; Rev. Nicholas Rafael, Greek Orthodox leader of ecumenical Holy Land pilgrimages; Pim Dodge, Methodist Lay Speaker and veteran host on Holy Land tours; Rev. Abuna Elias Chacour of Ibillin, Galilee, founder of Prophet Elias College, author of the widely-read *Blood Brothers* and Palestinian Christian promoter of reconciliation among Christians, Jews and Muslims; Monsignor Dr. Richard Mathes, Chargé of the Holy See and Director of Notre Dame of Jerusalem Center; Bishop Nicholas J. Samra, Palestinian Christian leader in the U.S.A.; kibbutz-raised syndicated financial advice columnist Susan Bondy; Palestinian advocate Rev. Naim Ateek of the Liberation Theology Center in Jerusalem, and my congenial editor, Alex Moore. I can truly thank the Lord this book did not go to press without their collective corrections and insights. Of course, I assume full responsibility for the final product.

Finally, I want to express my gratitude for the boost Rhodes & Easton publishers gave to the project by granting their 1996 Great Lakes Book Publishing Contest award to this book.

INTRODUCTION

My goals in writing this book are to motivate more Christians of all denominations to become pilgrims to the land made holy by God's special presence there and to help them to become better pilgrims and ambassadors of Christ.

Recent trips to the Holy Land have demonstrated the urgent need for a book like this one. Traveling, both independently and with tour groups, I have discovered how much one's pleasure and edification can be enhanced by arriving with a basic knowledge of the peoples, places and events of the Holy Land over the past four thousand years. Conversely, ignorance of ancient Israel, David's kingdom, the building and destruction of the temples, the early church in Roman Palestine, the Byzantine era, the Muslim conquest, the quixotic Crusader kingdom, the Ottoman Turkish era, the modern State of Israel and the Palestinian Arab people sorely limits one's ability to appreciate such a trip.

Time and again I found myself answering questions from fellow pilgrims about the most basic things. What were the Crusades? Are the Greek Orthodox Jews? Do the Muslims believe in our God? Who is this Constantine our tour guide talks about? How many Baptists live here? Are there any native Christians living in Jerusalem? Why is Tel Aviv so

Pilgrims carry a cross through the Old City on the Via Dolorosa. The author is at the foot of the cross. His pastor is at front left, their Palestinian Christian guide at front right.

prosperous and Joppa so poor? Why are there so many soldiers on the street? Who are these men dressed in black with long, full beards? (Answer: In the Holy Land they might be ultra-Orthodox Jews, Greek Orthodox priests, Benedictine monks or Druse.)

A typical Christian pilgrimage to Israel and the West Bank takes one to as many as forty sacred places associated with events in the life of Christ or of other persons in the Bible, such as Abraham, Rachel, Absolom, David, Elijah, John the Baptist, the Virgin Mary, Saint Peter and Lazarus. If we expect to be transported back to the world as it existed in Jesus' time, we are in for a shock. Calvary and the "empty tomb" do not look at all today as they are pictured in imaginative religious paintings. Both are now enclosed within the same ancient and ornate church in the heart of Jerusalem! It is best to be prepared for this shock. Then one can concentrate on the momentous fact that this is, indeed, the place of Jesus' crucifixion and resurrection.

There is much one can do to prepare for a pilgrimage. I have made a number of suggestions to enrich the experience, including a listing of hymns and Scripture readings appropriate to the holy places. Proper spiritual preparation can turn accidental tourists into purposeful pilgrims, and that is a fundamental distinction I hope I have made in this book.

A Christian contemplating a trip to the Holy Land should be aware of the glorious tradition of pilgrimage to Jerusalem and the holy places. Christians have been drawn here since earliest times to "walk in his footsteps." They have come in droves, thousands on foot across Europe and the Middle East, thousands in the holds of ships on the Mediterranean. They have realized their dreams of kissing the ground where he walked, of sitting on the hillside where he preached the Beatitudes, of weeping with him in the Garden of Gethsemane, of singing carols at the cave in Bethlehem, of renewing baptismal vows in the Jordan where John baptized Jesus. This book will do its best to situate the would-be pilgrim in this never-ending stream of Christians who have been drawn to the places made forever sacred by his presence.

The book you are about to read is decidedly *not* a standard guide book. Other books are available if one is interested merely in a description of each town and city, public transportation, weather, accommodations, restaurants and entertainment. Rather, what has been attempted is a book to prepare one to have the most fruitful spiritual experience possible. Along with that, and of equal importance, I have attempted an explanation of modern Israel's people: Jewish, Muslim and the amazing variety of Christian communities, both native and stemming from abroad. I hope that this information will not only increase the pilgrim's enjoyment but will facilitate interpersonal contact with all these groups of people, especially the beleaguered native Palestinian Christians.

My approach is unabashedly that of a Christian writing primarily for an audience of Christians of all denominations and traditions. One thing I have come to understand, though, is the impossibility of saying anything about the history of the Holy Land and its peoples and religions without offending some individual or group. I have tried to avoid slighting or unjustly offending any group, insofar as that is possible. Hopefully my respect for the traditions of the Eastern Orthodox, Roman Catholics and Protestants of all varieties will come through. I have sought to look at the Holy Land through Orthodox, Protestant and Catholic lenses and to convey the value of their varied ways of experiencing the holy places. Jesus prayed "that they may be one" (John 17:21). The church desperately needs to present a united front to the world. This book aspires to be an aid in that cause.

Finally, I hope to convey an attitude of love and respect for our Jewish and Muslim friends who comprise the mass of the people you will meet in the Holy Land. Both have endured much and have much to teach us. It is with enthusiasm that I introduce the reader to their world. Hopefully the reader will come home and use what has been learned in the Holy Land to increase world understanding. Jesus would be pleased if this once-in-a-lifetime spiritual odyssey increases respect for other cultures and peoples of other faiths. Even if you are an armchair traveler, may the reading of this book contribute to your appreciation of the peoples of the Holy Land.

There is talk of a summit of world religions on Mount Sinai or in Jerusalem in the year 2000 A.D. What a hopeful thought! Whether it happens or not, it is a reminder that this land is truly the most sacred place on the earth. If this great gathering does not happen now, may it happen in our lifetime. And may it bring our human race together in more ways than one.

As the old Jewish toast goes: "Next year in Jerusalem." And may our pilgrimages both strengthen our faith in Jesus and aid in the reconciliation of the peoples and religions of the Holy Land.

Jerusalem
and
the Holy Land

Part One

THE BACKGROUND

1.

A Short History
Of The Holy Land
From A Christian Perspective

Origins

According to Genesis, the first book of the Bible, Abraham was led by God to take his family from a place called Ur, located in what is now Iraq, and move to the land of Canaan (now the Holy Land) which was promised to his descendants forever. Abraham was the first of the Hebrew patriarchs, whose lives are recounted in Genesis. (The others are Isaac and Jacob.) They and their wives, Sarah, Rebecca and Rachel, belong to the oldest traditions of the Jewish people. They lived about 1900 B.C. and all but Rachel are buried in Hebron at the Cave of Machpelah.

The patriarchs and their descendants prospered in what we today call the Holy Land, but eventually they moved to Egypt because of famine. Most readers will recall the story of Joseph (about 1500 B.C.) being

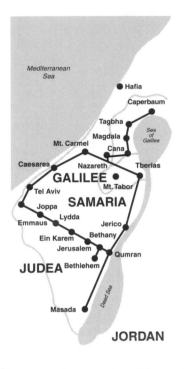

Places pilgrims are likely to visit.

sold into slavery by his brothers. He eventually became the Egyptian Pharaoh's chief advisor and administrator by virtue of his rare gifts and God's providence. The people eventually were subjected to persecution in Egypt, leading to the Exodus (about 1250 B.C.), led by that greatest of all Old Testament figures, Moses. While wandering in the desert between Egypt and Israel for forty years, the people were molded into a nation and received the Ten Commandments that Moses brought down from Mount Sinai. This prolonged, shared experience in the desert seems to have formed the people into a nation with a uniquely pure and monotheistic (one God) understanding of the divine.

THE KINGDOM OF ISRAEL

About 1200 B.C. the people crossed the Jordan River at Jericho (near where Jesus was later baptized by John) and returned to the "promised land." After a period of conflict with the native Canaanites and Philistines and other occupants of the land, they consolidated their control over the entire region. This was the era of the Judges, ending in the formation of a kingdom. David (about 1000 B.C.) was the most heroic of the kings of Israel. It was he who conquered Jerusalem, slaying the Jebusite inhabitants and making the area around Mount Zion his capital (the City of David). His son, King Solomon (960 B.C.), built a magnificent temple on Mount Moriah in Jerusalem for the worship of the God of Abraham, Isaac and Jacob. The nation prospered and extended its control over a wide swath of land, from the Mediterranean Sea in the west to the desert east of the Jordan, and from modern-day Lebanon in the north to the Sinai Desert in the south: as the Biblical expression goes, "from Dan to Beersheba" (north to south). (Judges 20:1; 1 Sam 3:20; 1 Chron 21:2.)

During the period of the kingdom, the oral traditions concerning the patriarchs, the sojourn in Egypt, the exodus and the giving of the Law were brought together in final written form. Moses himself was always understood as the divinely inspired author of the first five books of the Hebrew Bible, commonly known to Jews as the Torah and to Christians as the Pentateuch (Genesis, Exodus, Leviticus, Numbers and Deuteronomy).

The kingdom was split into the kingdoms of Judah in the south and Israel in the north after Solomon's death. The northern kingdom was destroyed by the Assyrians in 722 B.C., while the southern kingdom, including Jerusalem and the temple of Solomon were destroyed by the Babylonians in 587 B.C. These grave crises gave rise to the great prophets Isaiah, Ezechiel and Jeremiah, who constantly warned the people to repent and turn to God. During the Babylonian Captivity many of the writings of the Hebrew Bible were assembled in final form. It was a period of great spiritual activity.

537 B.C. UNTIL THE COMING OF CHRIST

After the return of the people from Babylon in 537 B.C., the nation never reached its earlier grandeur. At times it had autonomy, and a smaller version of the temple was rebuilt on the temple mount, but the dominant fact of life was foreign domination or outright rule, first by the Persians, then by Hellenistic rulers, and finally by Rome's great empire. Roman rule in Palestine, as it was then called, lasted for seven hundred years, from 63 B.C. until 636 A.D.

FROM CHRIST TO CONSTANTINE

About 20 B.C. King Herod the Great began rebuilding the temple on a magnificent scale. It was this temple to which Jesus was taken to be presented to the Lord God as a newborn. Here he edified the elders as a boy, preached during his public ministry, drove out the money-changers and prophesied its destruction and rebuilding in three days. By his day, pilgrimage to the temple was firmly established as a Jewish religious tradition. (Leviticus 23:1-44) Important feasts prompted great numbers of pious Jews to go "up" to Jerusalem. Jesus was among their numbers. His birth is estimated at 6 or 7 B.C. and his crucifixion and resurrection at 29 or 30 A.D. (Early Christian calculations of the date of his birth apparently were a few years off.)

The apostolic age, during which the gospels and epistles of the New Testament were composed and edited to their final form, lasted from Pentecost until about 100 A.D. During this time Christianity spread all over the Roman Empire, the "known world." In 70 A.D. a catastrophic event occurred for the Jewish people, the destruction of Jerusalem and the temple by the army of Rome after a revolt by Zealots.

In 135 A.D. the Emperor Hadrian crushed a second Jewish revolt, known as the Bar Kochba Revolt, banned Jews from the city, and rebuilt it, giving it a new Roman name, Aelia Capitolina. From that time forth the Jewish people wept, when they could, at the Western (or Wailing) Wall, the only remnant of the retaining wall of the glorious temple.

Deprived of their place of sacrifice, they spread all over the world in what is called the Diaspora (dispersion). But they never forgot Jerusalem.

The earliest Christian community in Roman Palestine was comprised of Jews who had accepted Jesus as the Messiah. They also must have suffered at the hands of the Roman rulers. The places of crucifixion and resurrection were deliberately covered over by great pagan temples to the gods of Rome shortly after 135 A.D. Christianity was suppressed until the Emperor Constantine's Edict of Milan (or Edict of Toleration) in 313 A.D., which began a three hundred year period of Christian civilization in Jerusalem and all of the Holy Land.

THE CHRISTIAN HOLY LAND

In the fateful year of 313 A.D. Constantine issued the Edict of Milan, ending persecution of Christians in the Roman Empire. For the next three hundred years Jerusalem was a Christian city and soon became a patriarchate, one of only five such major bishoprics in the world (the others being Antioch, Alexandria, Rome and Constantinople). This was done in honor of the sacred events which occurred there. About twenty years later, Constantine's mother, the Dowager Empress Helena, a fervent Christian, traveled with a great retinue to the Holy Land. With the help of the native Christians, she marked the sites of the major events reported in the gospels and built magnificent shrines over many of them. These included the Holy Sepulchre and the Nativity. From all over the Roman Empire, pilgrims made their way to Byzantine Palestine. During these centuries the country thrived as never before. It became the "Holy Land" to the Christian world. Every place associated with Christ or his mother or the apostles was venerated with intense feeling.

Not until modern Israel's rise in 1948 A.D. did the civilization of the

Christian pilgrims outside the 1300 year old Dome of the Rock, Islam's third holiest place, built on the ancient Temple Mount.

country again reach such heights. Artistic production, in the form of beautiful Byzantine-style churches, flourished. Thousands of Christian hermits took up residence in the Judean desert to the east and south of Jerusalem, while monasteries were built at Mount Sinai and other sacred sites. Saint Jerome produced his monumental Latin translation of the Bible in Bethlehem, making the scriptures available to all literate people in the West.

In 614 A.D. the Persians briefly occupied and destroyed much of Jerusalem, including the original Church of the Holy Sepulchre. To the Christian inhabitants this was as woeful a development as the Babylonian and Roman destruction of the two temples were to the Jewish inhabitants. The Holy Sepulchre was soon rebuilt, but not to its original grandeur.

THE ARAB PERIOD

In 636 A.D. the armies of Islam, the new religion energizing the nomadic tribes of Arabia, descended upon Byzantine Christian Jerusalem and, after a siege, conquered the city, beginning more than five centuries of Muslim Arab rule. For at least two or three of those centuries, Christians continued to constitute the majority of the people. Jews, in considerable numbers, returned to Jerusalem and Galilee. In general, both were tolerated by the ruling Muslim Arabs. Pilgrimage from Europe continued unabated, mostly on foot across three thousand lonely and dangerous miles.

About fifty years after conquering the region, the Muslim Arabs built two magnificent buildings on the temple mount, which had been a dumping ground for centuries. The Dome of the Rock is probably the most beautiful shrine in the Islamic world. It was built over the rocky outcropping on Mount Moriah believed to be the site of (1) the Jewish temple, (2) Abraham's preparations to sacrifice his beloved son, Isaac, at God's command, and (3) (according to the Koran, the Islamic holy book) the Prophet Mohammed's night journey from Mecca and his ascension into heaven. Muslims also believe the angel Israfil will sound the final trumpet there on Judgment Day. Nearby was built the Al Aksa Mosque. The two buildings and the temple mount area are, collectively, considered the third holiest place in the Muslim world, after the Arabian cities of Mecca and Medina. By this time Jerusalem had become a Holy City for the Muslims, as well as for the Jews and the Christians.

By the 900s A.D. Christian pilgrimages from Greece, the Balkans, Britain, France, Germany, Spain, Italy, the Low Countries and Scandinavia reached huge proportions, undertaken as a form of piety and atonement for sins. Despite the occasional mistreatment and gouging taxation by Muslim officials, there was no major cause for concern until 1010 A.D. when the mad Caliph al-Hakim thoroughly desecrated the great Church of the Holy Sepulchre, producing a shock wave of horror throughout Christian Europe. As the first wave of the Seljuk Turks took over control from the Arabs during the latter half of the eleventh century (1000s), repression of the pilgrimages became more blatant. Calls for a crusade to rescue the holy places from the unbelievers began to be heard in Europe.

THE CRUSADES

Because this era is being treated in a separate chapter, suffice it to say that Western European Christian armies invaded the Middle East and in 1099 A.D. captured Jerusalem and all of the Holy Land. They rebuilt Jerusalem and its many holy shrines and established the first European colony, which lasted for nearly a century. They held on to the fortified towns along the seacoast for a second century. During this two hundred year period, contact between East and West reached an intensity heretofore unknown. Western European Christians and Arab Muslims came into daily contact. The cultural exchange was earthshaking in terms of ideas and technology. The Crusader saga was both glorious and tragic, as will be illustrated in the chapter on the Crusades. In Catholic Europe's collective imagination this period became indelibly associated with chivalry, religious sentiments, adventure and nostalgia, kings and heroes and knaves.

THE ISLAMIC CURTAIN DESCENDS

From about 1300 until 1900, six long centuries, Christian access to the places where Jesus lived and died was severely restricted by Muslim governments. After the Crusades the region was ruled by Mamelukes from Egypt and Seljuk Turks. They were followed by the Ottoman Turks, who ruled from 1517 until World War I. Palestine, as the area was then called, became a backwater. The native Christian communities maintained a very low profile, and conversion to the dominant religion, Islam, caused a steady attrition. Jews and Christians were barely tolerated. At that, they probably fared better than did Muslims and Jews under the Crusader rule, sad to say.

Various Christian governments intervened to protect pilgrims and the holy places, especially the Holy Sepulchre and the Church of the Nativity in Bethlehem. Power politics were played repeatedly by France, Austria, Germany and Russia, each seeking advantages for their citizens and coreligionists. After the fall of the Christian kingdom of Jerusalem, Saint Francis of Assisi went to the area in a doomed effort to bring Christ to the Muslims. Although his efforts failed, he did leave considerable good will, and his followers, the Franciscan friars, became the main standard-bearers of the Latin, or Western, Church in the Holy Land. To this day, they are the custodians of many of the holy places where they can be seen in their familiar brown habits.

THE MODERN ERA

In 1917, the British General Allenby took Jerusalem from the Turks as World War I was coming to a close. This ended centuries of corrupt, absentee Turkish rule and oppression of Christian and Jewish minorities. Under a mandate from the League of Nations, Britain ruled Palestine until 1947. In that year, the United Nations partitioned the country between Israel and the Palestinians. The State of Israel was inaugurated in 1948.

A state of hostility immediately commenced between Israel and its Arab neighbors, Jordan, Lebanon, Syria, Egypt, Iraq and Saudi Arabia.

As a result of the war, the West Bank, East Jerusalem and the Old City came under Jordanian rule.

Wars were fought in 1948 and 1956. The struggle came to a head in the 1967 Six Day War, in which Israel seized the Sinai Desert from Egypt to the south, the Golan Heights from Syria to the north, and East Jerusalem (including the Old City) and the West Bank (Judea and Samaria) from Jordan to the east. Jews were once again able to worship at the ancient Western, or Wailing, Wall of the Temple Mount. Muslims continued to worship on the Mount itself at the Dome of the Rock and the Al Aksa Mosque, but under the watchful eye of Israeli soldiers. Since that time Israel has made peace with Egypt in 1979 and with Jordan in 1994. It began talks with the Palestinian Liberation Organization, conceding autonomy to some areas in 1995.

Israel's declaration of the newly-reunited Jerusalem as the "eternal capital" of Israel exacerbated tensions between Jews and the Arab population of Israel and the occupied West Bank, including Arab East Jerusalem. This led to the Intifadah, a period of violent confrontation between elements of the Palestinian populace and Israeli soldiers. Against all odds, a peace process commenced under patient prodding from the United States. Gradual home rule for the Palestinians, first in the Gaza Strip and Jericho, then in all the larger West Bank cities, was agreed upon. Where this will lead is unknown.

2.

Chronologies –
Getting Situated

Now that we have summarized the sweep of history in narrative form, it may be helpful to the reader to visualize major eras and critical events in the form of a chronology, which is easier to absorb. The first list is general; the second is more focused on Christian concerns. Note that many dates are rounded off or approximated for ease of retention.

GENERAL CHRONOLOGY

2000 B.C. Abraham and his tribe settle in present-day Judea; Jewish monotheism begins.

1500 B.C. Abraham's descendants, led by Joseph, settle in Egypt.

1250 B.C. Exodus from Egypt led by Moses. After forty years of wandering in the desert, Hebrews settle in land now called Israel.

1000 B.C. King David captures Jebusite city of Jerusalem and makes it Jewish capital. King Solomon builds first temple for worship of God. Era of prophets begins.

600 B.C. First temple destroyed. Captivity in Babylon. Jeremiah preaches repentance.

20 B.C. King Herod the Great starts to build second temple.

5 B.C-30 A.D. Life of Jesus Christ.

70 A.D. Second temple destroyed by Romans.

135 A.D. Jews dispersed throughout the world.

30-300 A.D. Christianity persecuted by Rome, but spreads.

313 A.D. Emperor Constantine legalizes Christianity, which quickly becomes dominant religion of Empire.

335-636 A.D. Era of Christian Byzantine culture in Jerusalem.

636-1100 A.D. Muslim Arab rule. Christian pilgrimages from Europe become a major phenomenon.

1100-1300 A.D. Crusades. Latin Kingdom of Jerusalem.

1300-1900 A.D. Egyptian and Turkish Muslims rule. Ottoman Empire.

1948 A.D. State of Israel inaugurated. Modern era begins. Wars between Israel and its neighbors: 1948, 1956, 1967, 1973.

Christian Chronology In The Holy Land

5 B.C. Jesus Christ born in Bethlehem, just outside Jerusalem.

26-30 A.D. Jesus' ministry in Galilee (northern Israel); apostles called, preaching and healing throughout the Holy Land.

30 A.D. Crucifixion and resurrection of Jesus. Descent of the Holy Spirit. Church begins.

30-100 A.D. Church spreads from Jerusalem throughout Roman Empire. Gospels and Epistles written.

100-300 A.D. Church becomes organized, clarifies its theology. Consensus develops on a Canon of divinely-inspired Christian Scripture. Periodic persecution by Roman government.

313-636 A.D. Emperor Constantine's Edict of Milan requires tolerance of Christianity. Christian religion becomes dominant in Roman empire. Byzantine (Greek) Christianity becomes dominant in Palestine. Great shrines built over multitude of places made holy by life of Jesus. Pilgrimages from Europe to Holy Land begin.

636-1099 A.D. New religion of Islam conquers Middle East. Christians continue to live in Holy Land after Muslim conquest, but in subservient position. Pilgrimages from all over Christian Europe become major religious phenomenon in Palestine.

1099-1291 A.D. Crusaders capture Jerusalem. Hold it until 1187 A.D.; calling the region the (Latin) Kingdom of Jerusalem. Holy Sepulchre rebuilt. East meets West. Widespread building of churches and castles throughout Holy Land. Western Europe becomes obsessed with Holy Land. Knighthood and chivalry focus on the defense of the holy places. Last Crusader stronghold, St. John of Acre, falls to Muslims in 1291 A.D., ending an era.

1300-1900 A.D. Christian pilgrimages continue despite oppression, but at greatly reduced rate. Franciscans become caretakers of otherwise abandoned Latin Christian shrines. Native Christian population (Greek Orthodox, Armenian, Coptic, etc.) suffers hardships but is tolerated by ruling Turks. Church survives in a sea of Islam. Jewish population begins to grow by immigration.

Twentieth Century Zionist movement, following World War II's Jewish Holocaust in Europe, culminates in 1948 establishment of present State of Israel. Official repression of churches ceases, but native Christians begin to emigrate in large numbers. Free access to all shrines and holy places after 1967 war. Beginnings of cooperation among leaders of rival native Christian churches. Intifadah (Arab uprising). Arab/Israeli peace process begins. Israeli government actively promotes tourism, including Christian pilgrimages. Palestine Liberation Organization (PLO) begins talks with Israel in pursuit of home rule and possible Statehood.

THE OLD CITY TODAY

N

Rockefeller Museum

Garden Tomb   Herod's Gate

MOSLEM QUARTER

Cemeteries

Cemeteries

CHRISTIAN QUARTER

Damascus Gate

Church of Saint Anne

Lions' Gate

Notre Dame Hospice

Ecce Homo Arch

via Dolorosa

Tomb of the Virgin Mary

Ethiopian Monastery

Tunnel

Haram al-Sharif (Temple Mount)

Dominus Flevit

New Gate

Greek Orthodox Patriarchate

Golden Gate

Gethsemane

Church of the Redeemer

Dome of the Rock

Mosques

Mount of Olives

Church of the Holy Sepulchre

Tomb of Absalom

Jaffa Gate

Western Wall

al-Aqsa Mosque

David's Citadel

Yeshiva Porat Yosef

Cemeteries

Tower of David

Mosque Hurva Synagogue

Dung Gate

JEWISH QUARTER

Govenment Tourist Office

Burnt House

Christian Information Center

Armenian Cathedral of Saint James

Ramban Synagogues

CITY OF DAVID

Armenian Museum

Four Sephardic Synagogues

ARMENIAN QUARTER

Zion Gate

Gihon Spring

Cemeteries

Tomb of King David and Room of the Last Supper

Brook of Siloam

Valley of Kidron

Mount Zion

Valley of Hinnom

3.

Pilgrimage – A Glorious Tradition

WHY PILGRIMAGE?

The phenomenon known as pilgrimage has a long and cherished history, not only in Christian life but also in Buddhism, Hinduism, Islam and Judaism; and, within Christianity, not only to Jerusalem but also to Rome, Canterbury, Chartres, Santiago de Compostela, Guadelupe, Lourdes, Constantinople, and many other shrines in Europe and the Americas. Marian shrines attract many thousands to France, Portugal, Mexico and Bosnia even today.

A recent Israeli government tourist pamphlet observed:

A pilgrimage to the Holy Land has long been enshrined in the traditions of the world's major monotheistic religions. Jews come to visit the tombs of the patriarchs and sages and the Wall of their ancient Temple. Christians come to retrace the footsteps of Jesus. Muslims come to worship at their holy shrines.

It is, then, important for a pilgrim of our day to situate oneself within this glorious tradition, to have a sense of being part of the movement of human history towards the Almighty; as we Christians like to say, to "walk in his footsteps."

Why the longing to see the holy places with our own eyes?

One might as well ask why Americans go to Pearl Harbor, to the beaches and military cemeteries of Normandy, to the fateful battlefields of Gettysburg, to the Lincoln Memorial, to the assassination spot in Dallas, to Mount Vernon, or to the Vietnam Memorial. Why do Jews and sympathetic Gentiles pay their homage at Auschwitz?

The answer is that we feel especially close to the people and events involved, our consciousness is raised and we can sense the reality of beloved people and events which come alive in a unique way.

JEWISH PILGRIMAGE

In the Hebrew religion of Jesus' time hundreds of thousands traveled to Jerusalem for Passover and other major feasts. (See Leviticus 23.) People traveled from the far flung Jewish communities "up" to Jerusalem to worship at the Second Temple. After the destruction of that Temple (70 A.D.), pilgrimage lost its sacrificial character and joyousness and became an emotional, heart-rending experience of sadness. For the next 1900 years pilgrims to the ruins of the retaining wall of the Temple came principally to mourn.

The gospel of John records a number of trips by Jesus to Jerusalem on the occasion of feasts. The Acts of the Apostles mentions that on the occasion of the first Christian Pentecost there were visitors in Jerusalem from all over the Mediterranean world, all Jews but speaking many languages. They were there to celebrate the Jewish festival of Pentecost (Fifty days after Passover). They were Parthians, Medes and Elamites, people from Mesopotamia, Cappadocia, Asia, Egypt and Rome. The tradition of Jewish pilgrimage has been revived and flourishes today in Israel.

CHRISTIAN PILGRIMAGE

The following passage from *Waiting for the Presence*, a beautiful little book by a pilgrim from Canada, Father Robert Wild, summarizes the appropriation of this tradition by Christians:

> From the earliest centuries Christians began to make their prayerful way to the sacred places where Jesus lived and suffered and appeared after His resurrection. They wanted to say thank you for His coming. They wanted to ask for a healing, or a special favor. Sometimes they went in reparation for their sins; or perhaps they simply sought a deepening of their faith. Whatever the reason, pilgrimage was one of the forms taken by Christian love and devotion.

Christian pilgrims from abroad began to travel to Palestine at least as early as the 200s. When Constantine erected the magnificent shrines over the newly-excavated sites of the crucifixion and the tomb of Christ in the early 300s, a steady stream of pilgrims began. Saint Jerome's writings about the holy places, while he was living in Bethlehem, increased the pilgrim flow in the 400s. Although traffic slowed after the coming of Islamic rule in the 600s, it picked up again in the 800s, climaxing in a thunderous beating of feet across Western Europe, the Balkans, Asia Minor and the Middle East, and back home again during the 900s and 1000s. While pilgrimage virtually ceased in northern Europe after the sixteenth century Reformation, it continued in the Catholic countries of southern and central Europe, and in the Orthodox nations, although it was discouraged by an uncooperative Ottoman Turkish government.

The early Protestant reformers generally condemned pilgrimage to holy places as without spiritual benefit, associating in with a form of spirituality they rejected. Many of northern Europe's own shrines, including the popular English shrine at Canterbury in honor of the martyred archbishop, Saint Thomas a Becket, were destroyed. Interest in travel to the Holy Land was rekindled among English, German and American Protestant groups in the nineteenth century.

Pilgrimage overland from Russia to the Holy Sepulchre started in a trickle shortly after the country was converted to Orthodox Christianity, about the year 1000. It gradually became a major theme in Russian spirituality, reaching its peak shortly before the 1917 Bolshevik Revolution.

MUSLIM PILGRIMAGE

It is important to realize that the apparently universal human attraction to one's holy places has a long history in Islam, as well as in Judaism and Christianity. The hajj, or pilgrimage to Mecca, is one of the five "pillars" of Islam, a religious duty for every Muslim who can afford the trip. The occasion is the Feast of the Sacrifice which occurs in the spring. Sheep, cows and camels are slaughtered by the millions as a sacrifice to Allah. Echoes of the ancient Jewish temple sacrifice of animals are obvious. The meat goes to the poor.

It is said that more than two million Muslims participate in the annual spring hajj. One million are domestic pilgrims from within Saudi Arabia, but more than a million come from around the world. The hajj begins with a prayer service on Mount Arafat. The people then walk the twelve miles to Mecca, wearing seamless white robes, stopping along the way to "stone the devil," casting pebbles at an ancient brick pillar standing in the desert. The simple robes symbolize the equality of all Muslims, an important tenet of the religion.

The pilgrims proceed to Mecca's Grand Mosque, Islam's holiest place, where these multitudes walk seven times around the sacred Kaaba, a cubic stone structure inside the Grand Mosque, and cut their hair. These rituals emulate a Seventh Century trek by Mohammed, Islam's prophet. After a week of prayer and recitation of verses from the Koran, the pilgrims visit other shrines. Illustrating the intimate relationship with Judaism, the slaughter of the sheep and other animals symbolizes the Hebrew patriarch Abraham's willingness to sacrifice his only and beloved son to God.

HARDSHIPS OF MEDIEVAL PILGRIMAGE

Western Christian pilgrimage to Jerusalem and surrounding Palestine reached its spiritual zenith during the 900s and 1000s, when it was primarily a means of atoning for sins already forgiven by God through the sacrament of penance, or confession. This led easily into the Crusades, envisioned as "armed pilgrimages." Jonathan Sumption, in his book *Pilgrimage, An Image of Medieval Religion*, gives details of this era, describing pilgrim dress, the dangers of travel, the custom of selling or giving away one's belongings and joining a monastery upon return to the West, the rise of hospices along the three thousand mile route and the Knights Templar and Knights Hospitalers who aided the Western pilgrims in the Holy Land and en route. He describes in fascinating detail the hazards of early medieval travel and the exhilaration of arriving at the long-sought destination. The mandatory side trip to the Jordan River, where pilgrims recommitted themselves to their baptism, immersing themselves while fully clothed, was a highlight.

After the Crusaders finally departed at the end of the 1200s, Western pilgrims traveled almost exclusively by sea because of the predatory behavior of the ruling Mamelukes and Turks who made it very difficult for Latin Christian groups to travel overland from Europe. The misery of the conditions in the small, overcrowded boats is graphically described in Sumption's book. The Muslim chieftains exacted excessive taxes when boats landed at Joppa (also called Jaffa) which is adjacent to modern Tel Aviv. More taxes were levied at the individual holy places.

Still, pilgrims continued to come in large numbers, largely due to the Venetian package tours. Whole fleets sailed from Italy in the spring, returning in the fall. From the 1200s to the 1400s, the Venetian ships and sailors were the best in the world.

By the 1500s the hostility of the ruling Ottoman Turks, not to mention the breakdown of law and order in backwater Palestine, nearly killed Christian pilgrimage. Only the hardiest continued to risk the journey. The Franciscans kept a lonely vigil at their holy places, providing hospitality to the beleaguered pilgrims and maintaining a tenuous Western presence at the holy places, sharing custody with the Greek Orthodox and the Armenians, both of whom had closer relations with the Ottoman court in Constantinople.

TO "SEE" AND TO "TOUCH"

Before Constantine there was little for pilgrims to see. "The tomb of Christ was buried beneath tons of dirt, and over it stood a pagan temple," according to Robert L. Wilken's book, *The Land Called Holy*. The cave in Bethlehem and the tombs of the patriarchs in Hebron could be visited, "but Jerusalem itself the preeminent site was hidden from view." All this changed when Constantine's excavators cleared away tons of earth to reveal the site of the crucifixion and the empty tomb of Christ.

During the three Christian centuries (the fourth through the sixth) people were drawn to Jerusalem "to *see* and *touch* the places where Christ was physically present, and to be able to say . . . 'we have gone into His tabernacle, and have worshiped in the places where His feet have stood,'" according to Wilken. In sermons preached in the new Basilica of the Holy Sepulchre Cyril of Jerusalem (a church father and the bishop of Jerusalem following the erection of the beautiful new shrines over Calvary and the Tomb of Christ) would say: "Others only hear, but *we* both *see* and *touch*."

Wilkens tells of one Peter of Galatia, a pilgrim from Syria, whose delight in the holy places "was like the pleasure a lover receives from gazing on the clothing or the shoes of the beloved. Wounded with love for God and longing to see God's 'shadow,' Peter took himself to those *saving places* where he could *see* the founts that gushed forth."

During these Byzantine centuries, the population of Jerusalem rose to over fifty thousand from a previous high of ten to fifteen thousand, according to Wilken. There were four times as many people living in the country as a whole during this period than in biblical times. Pilgrims, like tourists today, were good for business They came from all over the Christian world.

This cosmopolitan atmosphere was repeated during the medieval period of the Crusader Kingdom of Jerusalem. The German knight, John of Wurzbug, according to Wilken, spoke of "Greeks, Bulgarians, Latins, Germans, and Hungarians (in the city), Scots, Navarrese, Bretons, English, Franks, Ruthenians, Bohemians, Georgians, Armenians, Jacobites, Syrians, Nestorians, Indians, Capheturici, Maronites and very many others..." One is reminded of the gift of tongues in Jerusalem on the day of Pentecost.

Not until our present generation has this human polyphony been replicated in such diversity in Jerusalem.

Fʀᴏᴍ Mᴀɴʏ Nᴀᴛɪᴏɴs

Many nations have left their mark on Jerusalem as pilgrims, but Russian Orthodox pilgrims of the nineteenth century deserve special mention. Amos Elon, an Israeli writer, in his fascinating book *Jerusalem, City of Mirrors*, tells us that as many as twenty thousand Russian pilgrims "in a state of high excitation, would congregate in Jerusalem at Easter time alone. Their piety, if not poverty, demanded that they arrive on foot." Many walked from the distant interior of the Russian Empire. They crossed the Black Sea on the open decks of small steamers, were led like cattle across the Middle East, "offering no complaints, only endless murmurs of 'Glory to Thee, O God! Glory to Thee!'"

From Elon's description of these Russian peasants, they must have been a sight to behold:

> They came ashore at Jaffa, kissing the ground, crossing themselves profusely, singing hymns, while tears of emotion flowed from their eyes. They would call one another brat (brother), atets (father) or dyed (grandfather) according to what their relatives ages were. They walked everywhere, bathed in every sacred pool, approached every sacred site on hands and knees . . .

> They did not expect a miracle. The expected to return home as changed men and women; many, perhaps, did. Everywhere they went they sang hymns—and were pursued by . . . beggars. However poor they were, they still spared a kopeck or two for alms. Many observers noted their tenderness and constant good cheer.

> The deep spirituality and simplicity of these nineteenth century Russian pilgrims is beautifully illuminated in *The Way of a Pilgrim*, the daily reflections and prayers of a wandering Russian Orthodox pilgrim of the 1850s who longs to make the ultimate pilgrimage to the holy places in Jerusalem. This little volume, recently republished, is good spiritual reading.

Pilgrims in front of the Church of the Beatitudes.

Scandinavians, stalwart seafaring travelers, made their mark during the Crusades and as medieval pilgrims and have a presence in Jerusalem today, including the Swedish Christian Study Center. In addition to their prominence in the Crusades, the Germans have built major churches and hospitals in the Holy Land during the past century. Kaiser Wilhelm financed major Lutheran and Catholic institutions in Jerusalem.

The French presence began with Holy Roman Emperor Charlemagne's status as protector of the holy places and of the Western pilgrims, about 800. Godffrey of Bouillon led the first Crusade and became the first ruler of Christian Jerusalem in 1099. The Kingdom of Jerusalem was so dominated by the French that it was referred to as the Frankish Kingdom of Jerusalem, and Arabs referred to all Western Europeans as Franks for centuries thereafter. A singular presence today is the famous Ecole Biblique, a leading center of Bible study where the Jerusalem Bible was composed in this century.

Italy's Holy Land connection includes the transportation of centuries of Western pilgrims across the Adriatic and Mediterranean Seas, the papal sponsorship of the Crusades, and the "Custos," or custody of the holy places entrusted by the Pope to the Italian branch of the Franciscan Order for the past seven hundred years.

The English, inveterate travelers and sailors, began to visit the Holy Land via Gibraltar during the medieval period. They played one of the most important parts in the Crusade movement, Richard the Lionheart's exploits being merely the most dramatic. And, of course, they ruled what was then called Palestine, from 1917 until 1948, under the British Mandate of the League of Nations.

Two other Christian nations, long forgotten until they recently achieved independence from Soviet rule, played prominent roles in Holy Land history: Georgia and Armenia. The Armenian Church, in particular, has had a role far out of proportion to its size. In addition to being one of the three churches with major possessory rights in the Holy Sepulchre and Nativity churches, Armenians have their own quarter in the Old City of Jerusalem, along with Jews, Muslims and the balance of the Christians. They cling tenaciously to their vested rights in the holy places and have thus far remained somewhat aloof from other churches. Stay tuned. Things are changing fast in the relationships among the churches in Jerusalem, as described in Chapter 12.

ORTHODOX PILGRIMAGE TODAY

Orthodox, Protestant and Catholic pilgrimages today are quite distinct, all worshipping the same God but in different ways. Perhaps we can learn from one another's approaches.

"Traditionally, Greek and Cypriot (Orthodox) pilgrims come to the Holy Land in old age to prepare themselves for a good death," according to Glenn Bowman, a professor at the University of Kent at Canterbury and a specialist on the anthropology of pilgrimage. Bowman traveled with a number of Orthodox, Evangelical Protestant and Catholic tour groups and took note of their different characteristics. He subjected their spiritual practices to the critical eye of a social scientist and made some generalized observations. Orthodox, he says, prepare for pilgrimage by confessing their sins and seeking redemption. Having done that, they prepare themselves symbolically for entry into paradise by having their feet washed by monks of the Brotherhood of the Holy Sepulchre who often meet them at the dock or airport. Their symbolic renewal of baptism in the Jordan is seen as a "cathartic reunification with the divine image within them" which has, through a lifetime, become obscured. They fill their bags with "crosses, burnt candles, bits of flowers and small flasks of lamp oil" to take home.

Bowman notes how little interest the elderly Orthodox pilgrims from Greece seem to have in biblical and historical lectures on the significance of the places they are visiting. They are intent on rushing into churches and kissing the icons. For them, "the interiors of churches prefigure Paradise." Travels around the country to holy places are less important to the Orthodox than simply being present in Jerusalem during feast days, in the company of thousands of other Orthodox believers in Christ. (A sense of being part of the Communion of Saints?) These people seem very focused on their religious reasons for being in the Holy Land.

Orthodox tend to concentrate their pilgrimages around Holy Week and the feasts of the Assumption of the Virgin and the Exaltation of the Cross. The peak experience is to be present at the Church of the Holy

Sepulchre, known to the Greeks as the Anastasis (Resurrection), during the ancient ceremony of the Holy Fire on the night before Greek Easter, when thousands of pilgrims pass the Holy Fire from hand to hand, after the Greek Orthodox Patriarch's torch is lit inside the Empty Tomb.

It should be noted that an Orthodox priest from the United States who has led many pilgrimages takes exception to much of the above, pointing out that it would be hard to distinguish between the piety of elderly Greek pilgrims and elderly Italian pilgrims. Since Greece and Cyprus are so close to the Holy Land it is possible that less sophisticated people can afford the journey and bring a less-sophisticated appearing piety with them, as compared to the more affluent pilgrims traveling at much greater cost from Western Europe or North America.

CATHOLIC PILGRIMAGE TODAY

Bowman's interviews with Catholic pilgrim groups indicated these people come to the Holy Land for inspiration, to renew their faith in order to return home with a greater sense of purpose in life. Instead of a "cosmological celebration" of the Christian community in Christ, Catholics seem to be seeking individual spiritual rejuvenation. At each holy site the group reflects on the appropriate biblical passage, as well as on the history of the shrine itself. The traditional Way of the Cross on the Via Dolorosa (Street of Sorrows) in the Old City is the classic example of Catholic religious style on a pilgrimage, with a group moving from one station on Jesus' passion to another, reciting the Scripture passage, praying together and reflecting. Being at the traditional places where Jesus is thought to have carried his cross through the streets of Jerusalem is important to them, although not critical. In fact, it was only during the celebration of mass that Bowman observed the Catholic pilgrims displaying exceptionally strong emotion, including breaking into tears during the Communion. We may wonder whether those pilgrims were rushed through too many holy places in too little time, only having time to meditate when the group paused long enough for a worship service.

A fascinating merger of the Orthodox and Catholic pilgrimage traditions can be found in the Holy Land Society of Saints Peter and Andrew. This typically American group organizes pilgrimages jointly led by a Greek Orthodox priest and a Roman Catholic priest, both from Jamestown, New York. Christian unity is one of their goals. The Society's pilgrimages worship at both Orthodox and Catholic-sponsored holy sites, exposing each to the other's spiritual and liturgical traditions. This kind of initiative could be adopted across other denominational boundaries.

PROTESTANT PILGRIMAGE TODAY

The Protestant group Bowman describes is not typical of Protestants as a whole but represents an important segment of Evangelical activity in the Holy Land. He notes that Protestant devotions in the Holy Land tend to be disassociated from the ancient holy sites revered by both Orthodox and Catholics. "Protestants, in general, approach the Holy Land for the same inspirational reasons as Catholics," but they seek an "unmediated" relationship to Christ, not one "encumbered" by institutions and historic shrines over the holy places. They frequent the open country around the Sea of Galilee, or the natural setting of the Garden Tomb in Jerusalem "where they can imagine Christ *in situ* rather than monuments thrown up by two thousand years of devotion to his memory."

The Garden Tomb is a classic example. It is not the tomb of Christ, as once thought, but it includes a careful reconstruction of a first century garden, of a sort conjured up by a reading of the gospels. Above the garden is a rocky outcropping resembling a skull, not unlike the biblical description of the place of crucifixion. It is a peaceful, prayerful place. One can more readily imagine Jesus' death and resurrection here than inside the ancient Church of the Holy Sepulchre. Certainly the Garden Tomb appeals to our imagination and our sentimental and naturalistic impulses.

If one has any doubts about the "shrine" versus "natural setting" difference in *emphasis* between Protestant and Catholic pilgrimages, it should be enough to view Pat Boone's scenic Holy Land videotape and compare it to any produced under Catholic auspices. (Information on Holy Land videotapes is found in Chapter 14.)

Some evangelical groups are focused on the Second Coming; Jerusalem is a magnet for them. Christian Zionists are part of this movement, which received a great boost from Hal Lindsay's *The Late Great Planet Earth.* Their International Christian Embassy organizes pilgrimages to Jerusalem. Looking towards the "end times," they support the rebuilding of Solomon's Temple and enthusiastically, almost fanatically, call for a State of Israel reaching "from the Nile to the Euphrates." (That would encompass modern Egypt, Syria, Lebanon, Jordan and Iraq!) While fundamentalist and some other Evangelical Christian tour groups from Western nations have, in their zeal for Israel, looked askance at or ignored the native Palestinian churches, there is reason to believe this may change. Gary Burge, a theology professor at Wheaton College, has sought to raise Evangelical consciousness of the Arab Christians and their plight in his 1993 book *Who Are God's People in the Middle East?.*

While Evangelicals represent the part of Protestant pilgrimage which is farthest removed from traditional Orthodox or Catholic piety, even the more liturgical Protestant groups, such as Anglicans,

Lutherans and Methodists, tend to be less enthralled by the beautiful shrines than are Orthodox and Catholic Christians. But, as Bowman observes, "it is hard work for all pilgrims to cut through the din of the pilgrim buses, the clamor of the tour guides, and the thunder of heterodox forms of devotion to hear the small, still voice of God at the centre of the storm." The fact that Protestant pilgrimage groups have no place to hold formal worship services inside the historic shrines conditions their ability to appreciate such places. Chapter 12 will address this problem more fully.

Actual pilgrims, of course, may not be typical of their denominational group as a whole. Many Protestant pilgrims follow the Way of the Cross on the Via Dolorosa. Likewise, many Orthodox and Catholics feel closest to Jesus in the Judean Desert, at the Jordan River, up on the Mount of Olives overlooking the city, or on a hillside above the Sea of Galilee. In generalizing, we must always make room for the individual's unique response to the inspiration of the Spirit. There are also cultural differences from country to country at play here. Some observations may have more to do with social class than religious denomination.

TOURISM VERSUS PILGRIMAGE

In *Waiting for the Presence*, Father Wild graphically illustrates the difference between an attitude of pilgrimage and one of tourism:

> There is a great deal of tourism today which goes by the name of pilgrimage. Very often, attitudes of tourism and pilgrimage are mixed ....
> With this book I seek to deepen the interior attitude of pilgrimage, with the prayer that all tourists to sacred places may become pilgrims.

* * * * *

The beautiful Sea of Galilee.

These shrines are saturated with the presence of Christ, with the mysteries of His life and death and resurrection. It is of the very essence of pilgrimage to, like Jesus, linger, be present, enter into the divine atmosphere of the shrines. Our Western minds have lost much of our belief in sacred atmospheres.

I was praying in the Cave of Bethlehem one afternoon and a tour came through. After giving the usual little speech on the historicity of the site, etc., the guide said: 'And now, before we leave, *in order to cre-ate a little atmosphere*, let's sing one verse of O Little Town of Bethlehem.' If there's any place on earth we do *not* have to create any atmosphere it is in the Cave of Bethlehem! The Presence is there; the sacred mysteries saturate the air. **All we have to do is wait on the Presence, be present to the Holy.**

One afternoon, again in the Cave of Bethlehem, I was praying alone.

A young man, obviously an American, came in, dressed in shorts, with backpack, camera and all. He stood in front of the Crib with a rather pained and frustrated look on his face. After about five minutes he came over to me and said, 'Is this it?' implying 'is this all there is to it?'

Of his visit to the shore of the Sea of Galilee, Father Wild expresses his feelings of awe. May the reader find his attitude contagious:

Here was a miraculous catch of fish. Here the apostles recognized the risen Lord. Here the New Adam peacefully walked up and down the shore in the morning hours. Here was the reunion of Jesus with His friends, sitting with them around a charcoal fire as the sun rose over the lake .... As the hymn says, 'God and man at table have sat down.'

He demonstrates the spiritual imagination of the true pilgrim as he describes the experience of touching the water of the Sea of Galilee (also known in the Bible as the Lake of Gennesaret and designated on contemporary Israeli maps as Kinneret):

After getting settled in my room I went to the shore of the Lake. It was the first time I was able to touch the Lake, so I dipped my hand in and blessed myself. Jesus had walked on it, calmed it, perhaps even swam in it. It's still holy and always will be. I stood there on the shore. Even though it was afternoon I let the whole astounding episode of the Gospel wash over me like the waves that were now washing over the shore.

Because they are singularly inspiring, his reflections on two more wonderful places must be included here:

As I would do several times during my stay in Jerusalem, I climbed the Mount of Olives in the early evening and just walked around, or prayed, or sat on a rock overlooking the city of Jerusalem. Christ must have come up here hundreds of times and spent hundreds of hours in prayer. Because I believe my own vocation is praying for the world, this Mount became my favorite spot. Here is where Jesus prayed for the world and for the peace of Jerusalem. Here is where he pleaded with His

Father that the world would recognize Him. Here is where He taught us how to go apart and pray to the Father in secret.

*****

Not far from the church is Gethsemane .... You can't believe you're there, in these places you've been meditating on all your life. You see the centuries-old olive trees which date back to the time of Christ. You see, in the church, the huge rock where tradition says Jesus sweat His Blood.

Americans can feel patriotic anywhere, but pride in one's country rises in the breast at the Tomb of the Unknown Soldier or in front of the Lincoln Memorial. Likewise, Christians can pray anywhere, but nowhere is the atmosphere more conducive to reverence than at these sacred places, if we but use our spiritual imagination. That many pilgrims are deeply affected despite the distractions and hectic pace is evidenced by this reflection, written for a church bulletin by Irene Bush, a fellow pilgrim of the author, following her return from the Holy Land:

My eyes fill with tears when I think about this profound experience. I have been there. I walked the land where Jesus walked, up and down what seemed a thousand steps, steep hills and inclines, through beautiful valleys and ornate churches. And as I walked I thought about how Jesus must have traveled through this mountainous terrain with only a donkey as his transportation. I thought about how much he had accomplished and how profound an impression he made for all eternity in just three short years of ministry on earth.

It was a memorable journey and I am so grateful I had the opportunity to go. My life will never be quite the same again.

4.

The Crusader Kingdom
East Meets West

T he Crusades were a dominant cultural, political, economic and social force in Christian Europe throughout the two centuries of the High Middle Ages, 1100-1300 A.D. A comparable brooding presence in our lives of the past half century would be the Cold War, with its Soviet Communist menace and the specter of nuclear annihilation. Western Europe in the twelfth and thirteenth centuries was as obsessed with fear of Islam, love of chivalry and the gallant deeds of the Crusaders, and the duty to defend the Holy Sepulchre of Jerusalem, as America has in its recent past been obsessed with fear of World Communism, love of our nuclear arsenal, and the duty to defend the "Free World."

Amos Elon, in his book referred to earlier, *Jerusalem: City of Mirrors*, says "For centuries, Latin Europe remained obsessed with the story of Jerusalem and of the chiefs who had fought on her behalf: Tancred; Godfrey of Bouillon; Raymond, Count of Toulouse; Frederick Barbarossa; Richard the Lion-Heart; Saint Louis. Jerusalem represented the highest political ideal .... the recovery of the lost Holy Sepulchre."

To their apologists at the time, the Crusades were armed pilgrimages to protect Eastern Christianity from Islam and to rescue the holy places of the gospels from desecration. To their severest critics today, the Crusades were another episode in the tradition of Western imperialism, but especially bloodthirsty and intolerant towards their victims. To students of culture and economics, the unintended consequences of the Crusades are most significant: the exchange of technology and scholarship between East and West, the beginning of Western interest in the rest of the world, an increased sophistication in Europe, and a legacy of mistrust between East and West.

THE FIRST CRUSADE

By the 900s and 1000s, pilgrims from Western Europe were beating a three thousand mile path to the Holy Land by the tens of thousands for reasons of penitence, piety and adventure. In 1010 a terrible destruction was wreaked on the Christian shrines, including the Holy Sepulchre, by the mad Caliph Hakim. This news quickly spread throughout Europe, incensing public opinion.

In mid-century the new Turkish rulers of the Middle East began to block the overland pilgrim routes. As far away as England and France this was ominous news to great numbers of people who had already made the trip or who longed to do so. Palestine was not some remote place to them, such as Tibet might be to us. It was more like Europe to us, a place where a number of our friends have journeyed. More than that, it was viewed as a uniquely sacred place, the protection of which was seen as a matter of honor for all Christians.

When the Byzantine Emperor begged for help in warding off the Turks, Pope Urban II issued his famous call for volunteers at Clermont in France in 1095. The Pope was motivated primarily by a desire to aid the Eastern Christians of the Byzantine Empire in Anatolia (Asia Minor) and Syria, who had recently been overrun by the Turks. Rescuing the Holy Sepulchre was but a secondary motive, but Urban's call for armed pilgrims touched a nerve. Huge numbers dropped their plows and joined the Crusade, especially in response to the rabble-rousing speeches of Peter the Hermit. The peasantry joined up in droves, led by their lords and knights. The French, or Franks as they were called, were particularly ripe for adventure, as a great surge in population had left many able and energetic young men without land or much to do. And the religious fervor of Western Europe at the time has possibly never been surpassed, before or since.

Armies traveled from all over Western Europe, particularly France and Germany, to Constantinople, the staging ground on the Bosporus, the strait which, with the Dardanelles, separates Europe from Asia. There followed military campaigns in Anatolia and the siege and capture of Antioch, then finally Jerusalem in 1099. The remnant of the defenders, about five thousand, were slaughtered, a fact pointed out endlessly by writers seeking to brand the Crusades as an unmitigated moral disaster.

There is, of course, no moral defense to be made for the slaughter of enemies under any circumstances, but a few points need to be made as a matter of perspective. First is the ugly fact that most of the many conquests of Jerusalem have been followed by the slaughter of the remaining defenders and citizenry. The Bible itself contains its share of gloating reports of slaughter, including the slaughter of the Jebusites when David conquered Jerusalem. The Romans slaughtered the Jews in 70 and 132 A.D. While the Arabs showed some restraint when they captured the city from the Byzantines, Islamic armies have not been known for restraint. Slaughter of enemies after victory is one of the horrible realities of war. The "civilized" rules of modern warfare, contained in the Geneva Convention, prohibit torture or slaughter of prisoners, yet the twentieth century has witnessed by far the greatest number of war-inflicted deaths in history. Perhaps a hundred million in all!

In earlier times winners had two choices if they intended to occupy the conquered city: make the defenders and their women and children and elders slaves or put them to death by the sword. Neither was a pleasant fate for the victims. Where, as in the case of the First Crusade, the conquerors were few in number and surrounded by a populous and hostile civilization, they undoubtedly would have felt threatened by an unfriendly Muslim and Jewish population within the city. It is amazing how conquering armies have been able to dehumanize the vanquished foe, particularly when the foe is of another religion or race. Medieval Europe was hopelessly intolerant of non-Christian cultures, seeing them as an affront to God. Tragically, this has been typical of the world until recent times.

Godfrey de Bouillon, the brave and modest leader of the conquest of Jerusalem, died the following year, and his brother Baldwin was crowned the first King of Jerusalem on Christmas Day, 1100. In a short time the Crusader Kingdom included all of the Holy Land, from the Jordan to the Mediterranean and from Syria to the Sinai Desert.

THE SECOND CRUSADE

In time the Westerners, mainly Franks, who took up permanent residence and raised families "went native." They began to mix with the Muslim Arabs, whom they called Saracens. They traded with them and even formed alliances against common enemies. Newly-arriving pilgrims and knights from Europe were appalled at the presence of Muslims within Christian Jerusalem. Within a couple of generations the inhabitants of the Kingdom of Jerusalem and the surrounding Christian principalities, known collectively in French as Outremare (Overseas), came to realize they needed peace to survive in an Islamic world. Unfortunately, more intolerant voices prevailed and war broke out again.

This time the Saracens were well prepared and brilliantly led by a new leader, a Kurd known to history as Saladin the Conqueror. The young king of Jerusalem made some tactical errors, engaging Saladin's army under a blistering sun, defending a hillside with no water to drink. Eugene Hoade, O.F.M., reports in his authoritative *Guide to the Holy Land*: "The flower of the Latin Kingdom fell at the battle of Hattin (July 15, 1187), and Jerusalem surrendered on October 2. Nothing was left of the Latin Kingdom by 1189 except Tyre, and to the north Antioch and Tripoli."

In less than a century a thriving Western enclave was crushed. Beautiful castles and churches and prosperous towns had been built. Foreign relations had been established with surrounding rulers. Commerce had flourished with Europe. All of this was lost.

THE THIRD CRUSADE

In all, there were eight Crusades, but the first three were the most significant for Jerusalem. The knights rallied and defended Tyre and regained other coastal strongholds after Hattin. A call went out in Europe for help. The great German Emperor Frederick Barbarossa was drowned on the way. The French were led by King Philip, the English by the great King Richard the Lion-Heart, or Coeur de Lion. He and Saladin were the great protagonists. Father Hoade reports that "During this Crusade the Christians and Muslims began to fraternize as they had never done before." Negotiations were held between Richard and Saladin over reestablishment of limited Christian rule in the Holy Land. Father Hoade quotes from Baha-ad-Din, a Muslim writer of the time, describing an exchange between the two regarding the importance of Jerusalem to each side:

> King Richard began: The points at issue are Jerusalem, the Cross, and the land. Jerusalem is for us an object of worship that we could not give up even if there were only one of us left. The land from here to beyond the Jordan must be consigned to us. The Cross, which for you is simply a piece of wood with no value, is for us of enormous importance.
>
> Saladin replied: Jerusalem is as much ours as yours. Indeed it is even more sacred to us than it is to you, for it is the place from which our Prophet made his ascent into heaven and the place where our community will gather on the day of Judgment. Do not imagine that we can renounce it. The land also was originally ours whereas you are recent arrivals and were able to take it over only as a result of the weakness of the Muslims living there at the time (i.e., of the first Crusade).

Needless to say, nothing was resolved. The two sides could not compromise their perceived superior sacred rights. They were constitutionally unable to empathize with the other. A fatal flaw for the Christians. With insufficient reinforcements and a slowing of Western immigration, the cause was ultimately lost by the small nation vastly outnumbered by its neighbors. Outposts were held for a century after the loss of Jerusalem, until the last bastion, Acre, fell in 1291.

In *The Source*, James A. Michener imaginatively describes a visit by
Volkmar, a leader of one of the great Crusader families, to the holy
places of Galilee. This took place shortly before the loss of Acre. It
poignantly reveals the deep sense of loss for all Christendom:

> Let the storks head for Germany, Volkmar said to himself. What
> man would leave this paradise? And he determined to stay on his land.

> At Nazareth, which seemed a sturdy anchor of Christianity in a
> land already become infidel, Volkmar left the others and went alone to
> the grotto where the archangel Gabriel had announced to the Virgin
> that she was to become the Mother of Jesus. It was a portentous spot,
> more nearly a deep cave than a grotto, and its walls were damp. As
> Volkmar stood in the narrow space the actual presence of Mary and
> Gabriel was made manifest. It was for this that the Germans, the
> French and the English had fought: that the Christian world might
> come in peace to such sacred spots and worship; but after two hun-
> dred years of warfare a knight of Ma Coeur could come to this holi-
> est of spots only on sufferance of a Mameluke slave. What had gone
> wrong? Why had the various Volkmars been unable to hold Nazareth,
> or the Baldwins, Jerusalem? Why should the scenes of our Lord's pas-
> sion be in infidel hands, lost forever to the Christians? He could not
> understand, and he lowered his strong head and whispered, 'Mary,
> Mother of God, we have failed you. For some reason I cannot com-
> prehend we have failed and soon we shall be driven away. Forgive us,
> Mary. We did not find the way.'

Michener's imaginative narrative continues:

> They rode then to Mount Tabor, where the appearance of Jesus
> had been transfigured from that of an ordinary mortal into the reality
> of a deity, and they stayed with the monks who ignored Mameluke
> threats and operated on top of the mountain; and next day they rode
> to the gentlest of the holy places, Cefrequinne, the Cana of Bible
> times, where a Muslim and his wife showed them the very cot on
> which Jesus had rested during the wedding feast. Young Volkmar

asked in Arabic if he might lie on the Lord's couch, and the Muslim replied, 'For one coin anyone may lie on it,' and the boy did so.

* * * * *

What had been the deciding point in the Crusades? Volkmar wondered as he stood in the house at Cefrequinne. When had failure become inevitable? He supposed it must have been at some unrecorded date early in the 1100s, in the time of Volkmar II, when it became obvious that no great number of European settlers were going to make the long trip to Jerusalem. We never had enough people, the count mused. How often do we hear of this king or that whose wife died or whose sons wasted away with no one coming along to take their places? We were always so few... so few.

* * * * *

How had men so essentially good in heart permitted catastrophes like Reynald and his kind? Than the saintly Louis, the French king in Acre, there could be no sweeter man; and the greatest of them all, Baldwin IV of Jerusalem, who, when his body was rotting away with leprosy and his eyes were blind and his feet gone, insisted still upon being carried into battle one last time against Saladin, whom he had defeated time after time.

* * * * *

If, after the First Crusade, we had never allowed another knight on this soil, Volkmar decided, but if we had brought instead farmers and shoemakers, we could have held the kingdom.

* * * * *

Nor did we achieve an alliance with the Arabs, binding their land to ours. So in the end Syria combined with Egypt and we were left an enclave on the edge of the sea. He reflected on the lost glories and concluded: We produced men of vision like Volkmar the Cypriot, but whenever they were about to effect some kind of compromise new fools landed from Europe to slay the Arabs and to destroy what the wise men were attempting.

*****

We needed the settlers from Europe ... couldn't exist without them. But all we got were warriors determined to kill the very friends we had to depend on for survival. Ah, well. He sighed ruefully and assembled his men for the ride to the Sea of Galilee.

The heroic but tragic and flawed Latin Kingdom of Jerusalem affords us an eerie but interesting parallel to the modern State of Israel. The centuries of longing to return to a beloved Holy Land from which a religion had been expelled. A series of catastrophic events prompting the Western Christian nations to support the creation of a theocratic state in the midst of Palestine. Many of the local Arab inhabitants are displaced. They are viewed contemptuously by the new rulers. An outburst of creativity builds up the brave new nation. A series of wars with neighbors preoccupies the new country. Faltering attempts to persuade coreligionists from abroad to immigrate in sufficient numbers. A failure to achieve peaceful coexistence with the Palestinian Arabs. Inability to resolve hostility with neighboring Syria. The flourishing of a culture and language unknown in the region for centuries.

The parallels are many. In the case of the Kingdom of Jerusalem, we know how it was destroyed by its enemies after eighty-eight years. One fervently hopes and prays that the long-range outcome is different this time!

There are profound contrasts, as well as parallels, between the twelfth century Latin Kingdom of Jerusalem and the twentieth century State of

Israel, which give hope for the long-term survival of Israel. For one thing, the moral justification for Israel's formation is on more solid footing. Also, Israel is militarily much stronger vis-a-vis its neighbors than was the crusader kingdom. Finally, Israel has developed an infrastructure and an agriculture to a degree impossible in the Middle Ages. It is very firmly entrenched in the land. May its strength lead to the compromises it must make if it is ever to achieve a lasting and true peace with the other people who have resided in the land for so many centuries. Empathy with the dispossessed Arabs was lacking among the Crusaders. It is also lacking in parts of Israeli society. It may be a crucial ingredient in a long-term peace.

Part Two

VISITING THE HOLY PLACES

5.

Christian Holy Places
"Where Jesus Walked"

AUTHENTICITY

From earliest times there has been debate about the authenticity of the particular sites venerated, and about the value of venerating Christ in the Holy Land as opposed to staying at home and worshipping God who is, after all, omnipresent. The feeling of the early pilgrims is expressed in this passage from *The Land Called Holy*, by Robert L. Wilken:

> For what set this land apart from all others was that God had been present not once or twice, not in one age or to one person, but in many ages and to many people—to Abraham, Moses, Elijah, in the desert, on the mountains, in the towns and cities, at the time of the Exodus, in the age of the prophets, during the time of the Maccabees, and, of course, preeminently in the life and suffering of Jesus of Nazareth.

Pilgrims praying in the Chapel of Calvary in the Church of the Holy Sepulchre.

In *Waiting for the Presence*, Father Wild expresses a sensible attitude towards the desire to ascertain the precise spot where the great biblical events happened:

> The question of whether this or that place was the actual, exact site of Christ's passion, birth, etc., never bothered me. As I descended to the Lithostrotos some maps and archeological evidence appeared on the walls. I didn't stop to look. It didn't matter to me. Let the archaeologists worry about it. It's a real temptation for the pilgrim to allow the problem of 'Is this the exact spot?' to disturb your mind.
>
> I believe in the Incarnation. I believe this is the Holy Land and this is the Jerusalem where He suffered. The sacred drama happened here somewhere. The whole land is holy. I would kiss every inch of it; I would gladly kiss every stone of every pavement uncovered.
>
> The same with His birth and the other events of His life. He really

was born in Bethlehem, so there's a holy cave there somewhere. The
whole Sea of Galilee is holy because He walked on it and calmed it. Its
whole shoreline is holy because He got in and out of boats somewhere.
Every mountain in Palestine is transfigured because He was transfigured
on one of them somewhere. Every hill is blessed because on one of
them, somewhere, He said, 'Blessed are the poor ....'

Despite the disclaimer, Father Wild's ability to focus on a particular
holy event or mystery while at the traditionally acknowledged site **does**
seem related to his acceptance of its authentic connection with Jesus.
While we can pray and meditate anywhere, it **does** make a difference
that we are at the real, honest to God places! They evoke an outpour-
ing of spiritual emotion which many people take home with them and
which seems to enrich their prayer life and their appreciation of the Bible
for many years.

To quote again from Father Wild:

> What else is appropriate when you arrive for the first time in your life
> **at the place where Christ was mocked as a fool for love of you!** I
> kissed the pavement many times. I knelt and prayed. I sat for several
> hours, meditating and praying and being present to the Holy.

Romantics may react to the Holy Sepulchre the same way Russian
writer Nikolai Gogol did, according to Elon's *Jerusalem: A City of
Mirrors*:

> He was repelled by the gaudy decor and the glossy marble. Like so
> many pilgrims before and after, he reflected how much more moving
> the crypt would have been had it been left a naked rock, starkly bare, a
> hole gaping in the dark.

Some have been so repulsed by the Holy Sepulchre's eclectic decor
and atmosphere that they search for another place which might prove
to be more "authentic." The most notable example is the Garden
Tomb, sometimes derisively called Gordon's Calvary. It is located out-

side the Damascus Gate. In the late nineteenth century the British General Gordon became convinced, after a dream, that here was the true place of crucifixion and burial of Jesus. It lay outside the city walls and seemed to conform to the gospel description of Golgotha, the "skull place." Gordon's reasoning in selecting the site of Calvary was shaky, to be charitable. He pictured an imaginary skeleton figure stretched out over the city and located Calvary in this way. As it turns out, he was deluded. Nevertheless, a lovely garden was developed around an ancient tomb, with a skull-shaped rocky area close by.

Isabelle Bacon, the Protestant author of *A Pilgrim Guide to the Holy Land*, describes the aesthetic merits of the Garden Tomb as a place of pilgrimage:

> The tomb which dates from the first century is one of a number of ancient sepulchres in the area. It is adjoined by a lovingly-tended garden and provides an excellent visual aid. *Sadly for many pilgrims however, there is no historical or archaeological evidence to support the validity of the site*, but it undoubtedly appeals to the imagination and is aesthetically more pleasing than the Church of the Holy Sepulchre.
>
> This peaceful haven from the busy streets outside is well worth a visit. A most suitable place in which to reflect upon the events of the first Easter morning.

*****

> Here one sees an empty tomb with the stone rolled away, as at Jesus' tomb. There are lovely trees in the garden, and here is a wonderful place to read one's Bible, to meditate and feel the crucifixion. Most people feel it better here than in the Church of the Holy Sepulchre.

Catholic and Orthodox pilgrimages have not visited this inspirational place, scorning it as simply a fake, and the tombs in the area apparently are a few centuries earlier than the time of Christ. This place once may understandably have been seen as an affront to the Holy

Sepulchre, where Christians have kissed the spots of the crucifixion and resurrection for nearly two thousand years. Today it makes better sense to see the Garden Tomb as an oasis for prayer and meditation in the bustling city, a place where one can readily conjure up images of the sacred happenings, an aid to our spiritual reflection. If Protestants are to be welcomed to worship in the holy shrines built over the actual holy sites, perhaps Catholics and Orthodox should consider visiting the Garden Tomb. It must be viewed, though, as an aid to spiritual reflection, not as the actual place of the death and resurrection of Jesus, which it certainly is not.

BETHLEHEM

As early as the second century, according to *The Land Called Holy*, Christians began visiting the cave in Bethlehem. The authenticity of the traditionally revered spot is supported by "a very strong and unchallenged tradition," according to *A Pilgrim Guide to the Holy Land*. The existing church, built by the Emperor Justinian the Great over the ruins of Constantine and Helena's church, dates from the 500s and is Christendom's oldest complete church still standing intact.

Isabelle Bacon makes the following case for the authenticity of the Church of the Nativity in Bethlehem and the cave beneath it:

Certainly local people would have remembered the birth—not least the shepherds who must often have been asked by their children, and their grandchildren, to tell the story of how the angels appeared to them on that first Christmas night. Their descendants would have known exactly where the birth took place.

The visit of the Magi must also have been a memorable event.

The oral tradition was undoubtedly very strong and in AD 135 the Roman Emperor Hadrian, perhaps to divert attention from the site, gave orders that a grove dedicated to the pagan god Adonis, should be planted in the immediate vicinity of the cave. If, as Saint Jerome sug-

The Cave of the Nativity in Bethlehem.

gests, this really was his intention, in effect he marked its location for the next two hundred years. The earliest written reference to the Bethlehem cave, surrounded by a grove dedicated to Adonis, was made by the Christian missionary Justin Martyr in AD 155. The writer Origen also confirms the same tradition in AD 215.

In 315 the Emperor Constantine, having been converted to Christianity by his mother Saint Helena, directed that a magnificent Basilica should be erected over the cave.

The same argument can be made in support of many of the revered sites in the Holy Land. They ought to be given the presumption of authenticity. Otherwise we would be assuming that Jesus' first century followers would not have come to these places for prayer in remembrance of him, and would not have marked them in some way and passed down the tradition until the end of the age of persecution.

THE MOUNT OF OLIVES

One of the most impressive places visited on most pilgrimages is the Mount of Olives overlooking the city of Jerusalem. Here Jesus frequently retired to pray to his heavenly Father. Here his triumphal "Palm Sunday" entry into Jerusalem began. Here is the garden of Gethsemane, where he prayed while his disciples napped the night before he died. Here is the site of his ascension into heaven. It affords us a magnificent vista of the Old City, as it did for Jesus when he wept over the city. Pilgrims ought to spend as much time here as possible, maybe arranging to visit in the evening after the day's activities are done. Here we may fittingly pause and pray for the City of Jerusalem, as Jesus did. (Matthew 23:37.) The Church of All Nations and the church called Dominus Flevit (The Lord Wept) are extraordinarily beautiful places for quiet meditation on the Mount of Olives.

THE UPPER ROOM

The "Upper Room," or Cenacle, is at once a place of awe and disappointment. Here on Mount Zion is the place of the Last Supper and the institution of the sacrament of the Body and Blood of Christ. It is also the place where the apostles waited in fear after the crucifixion, the place where Jesus twice appeared to them after the resurrection, and the place where the Holy Spirit descended upon the apostles in tongues of fire on the first Pentecost. Yet regular Christian worship has not been permitted in the room for centuries. It is certain that the present room is of medieval construction. It is stark, unadorned, unfurnished and neglected. Yet, it is probable that it is at least the approximate spot where the original "Upper Room" stood.

Constantine must have had good reason to erect a major church on Mount Zion at this spot in the fourth century, but the present "Upper

Room" itself must be appreciated as symbolic. Father Hoade, in his carefully researched *Guide to the Holy Land*, gives us this assurance of the authenticity of the site itself:

> There is no doubt that the house of the Last Supper became a church-synagogue for the Judaeo-Christians, and did not pass to the gentile Christians until the time of Constantine. A basilica was erected there by Archbishop John (386-417). Burned by the Persians in 614, the "mother of all churches" was restored by Modestus.

A nearby spot is considered by some to be the burial place of King David, although it may in fact be a very early Judeo-Christian synagogue. Christians, as well as Jews, visit David's Tomb, as well they should. Pilgrims are amazed to see a Muslim minaret on top of the building! This place is also holy to adherents of Islam, who, to a degree, incorporate Jewish and Christian revelation into their sacred belief system. It is thought by many scholars today that David is buried in the "City of David" area now being excavated.

Perhaps because it is both a mosque and a place of Christian veneration, the Upper Room has been closed to public worship for a long time. The Franciscan monks, who resided on Mount Zion throughout the centuries of Turkish repression, are allowed to lead a pilgrimage here on Holy Thursday and Pentecost Sunday. The pilgrims are permitted to pray and sing. There is reason for hope that public worship in the Upper Room may become more common. A bulletin of the Latin Patriarchate reported on a joint prayer service held there by Anglicans, Latin Catholics, Greek Catholics, Greek Orthodox, Ethiopians and Copts on the occasion of the Week of Christian Unity held in January of 1995. Such things have a way of becoming annual events.

Until pilgrims are allowed to celebrate the Eucharist, or Lord's

Supper, when they visit this uniquely eucharistic place, they might consider quiet prayer, reading of the gospel account of the Last Supper, and a "spiritual communion."

TOMB OF THE VIRGIN MARY

All that is left of the fourth century Church of the Assumption on the Mount of Olives is the crypt (underground sanctuary), reached through a Crusader arched doorway and a descent of forty-four steps into a dark, dungeon-like but very atmospheric church. The crypt is said to be the oldest religious building in Jerusalem. The fact that one may pray at the traditional site of Mary's tomb is certainly reason enough to visit this crypt church. Guarded, on alternate days, by Greek Orthodox and Armenian monks, it is used for formal worship by the Armenian, Greek, Coptic and Syrian churches. There is also a prayer niche, or mihrab, for Muslim worship, as they have a special reverence for Mary as the mother of the "Prophet Jesus." As described by Isabelle Bacon, "Hanging from the ceiling are a myriad of gold and silver lamps, while around the walls are many icons and other religious paintings. The roof has been blackened over the centuries by the use of candles ...." This holy place is a good test of our acceptance and embrace of diverse cultures and ways of expressing love for our God. It helps to know that it has been a place of Christian worship since the 300s!

SAINT PETER IN GALLICANTU

Of all the holy places in Jerusalem, this one is singled out here as a good example of the tortured history and antiquity of most such sites. This church on Mount Zion commemorates Peter's denial of Jesus three times "before the cock crowed." The word "Gallicantu" means "cock crow." No doubt the early church mentally marked the courtyard where Jesus was brought before the high priest, in order to perpetuate the memory of his public humiliation.

A major church was built at this spot in the fifth century by the Empress Eudocia. It was damaged in 529 during the Samaritan Revolt, destroyed in 614 during the Persian invasion, rebuilt around 628 by the Byzantines, cared for by Armenian monks during the early Muslim period, destroyed again in 1009 by the mad Caliph Hakim, rebuilt about 1100 by the Crusaders and cared for by Greek monks, destroyed again in 1219 by the Turks, replaced by an oratory (a place for prayer) which was destroyed around 1300, and most recently rebuilt in the 1920s by the Assumptionist Fathers, who maintain it today for the general public. This mind-boggling history is typical of so many Holy Land religious places. Today it is a beautifully decorated church, open to all.

Jordan River Baptismal Site

Since early times, Christian pilgrims to the Holy Land have included in their visit a trip over to the Jordan River to be "rebaptized" where John baptized the Lord (more correctly a *recommitment* since one can be baptized only once). This was also the approximate site where the Children of Israel entered Canaan after wandering in the desert for forty years. (Josh. 3:14-16.) It became a holy place for Israel.

The Byzantines built the Monastery of Saint John (the Baptizer) here and pilgrims flocked to the place called Oasr ol Yehud. Since then, millions have renewed their baptismal vows here, donning white robes and undergoing total immersion in the mild water of the river.

Due to hostilities between Israel and Jordan beginning in 1948 this traditional site of Jesus' baptism became off limits and surrounded by barbed wire. The ritual was moved north to a place called Yardenit, a Jordan River site maintained by a kibbutz. With peace reestablished between Israel and Jordan, the ancient site is being reopened, a cause for celebration by all Christians.

MOUNT TABOR

This is the most likely site of Jesus' Transfiguration, together with Moses and Elijah, in the presence of Peter, James and John. According to the early church father Origen, the tradition that this epiphany happened on this particular mountain goes back to apostolic days. There has been formal worship on top of the mountain, when permitted by law, at least since the Emperor Constantine's Edict of Milan (313 A.D.) ordered an end to Roman persecution of Christians.

Churches have been built and destroyed periodically ever since. The Franciscans, who have been official "custodians" of Latin Christian interests in the Holy Land since the Middle Ages, kept a lonely vigil on the mountain during the centuries when the Turks did not permit a church. Today there is a Franciscan monastery, a pilgrim hostel and a fine basilica commemorating Jesus' Transfiguration on the mountain top. The Greek Orthodox also maintain an historic church on Mount Tabor. It also should be visited, if possible, while on the mountain.

The mountain top is reached by a mildly-harrowing, twisting road, featuring several switch backs. The timid will not want to watch where they are going. The adventurers will love it. Fortunately, professional drivers take pilgrims up the mountain. It has been said: "Tabor rises up to heaven like an altar that the Creator built to Himself."

Father Hoade cautions us:

> The wonderful panorama one can enjoy from the top of Mount Tabor should be looked at with the Holy Scriptures in hand. Then to our eyes it will appear not as a vision of material things and the beau-

Renewing marriage vows at the Wedding Church in Cana of Galilee (friends of the author).

ty of nature but rather as a vision of centuries and ancient peoples: a vision of great events, of the greatest indeed, which history records.

GALILEE

Most pilgrimages and tour groups go to Nazareth, Cana, Capernaum, Tabgha and Tiberias, all in Galilee. The Sea itself, with the Golan Heights as its backdrop, must have been a great source of enjoyment to Jesus. It is remarkably beautiful and unspoiled by development. The opportunity to cross the Sea of Galilee is offered to most pilgrimage groups. This is a spiritual experience not to be missed, in addition to being a lot of fun. Here Jesus walked on the water, multiplied the loaves and fishes, preached the Sermon on the Mount and cooked breakfast for his fisherman disciples after his resurrection.

Because this book is not intended as a tour guide in the usual sense, we will content ourselves here with a more detailed description of just one of the many places worth visiting in Galilee: Cana. The town now known as Kefer Kanna has been considered the biblical Cana since Byzantine times. Here Jesus turned water into the finest of wines, at his mother's intercession, for the benefit of the wedding guests. This was his first recorded public miracle. Ruins in Kefer Kanna indicate the existence of a Jewish-Christian church, in the synagogue style, dating to the 200s. Today there is a sizable Palestinian Christian population in the town. What is unique to the lovely "wedding church" at Cana today is the practice of couples on pilgrimage renewing their marriage vows. Marriage Encounter pennants from many countries, autographed by thousands of couples, line the walls. Orthodox and Catholic churches commemorating the miracle stand close to one another.

OTHER HOLY PLACES

There are many holy places beyond the scope of a first visit to the Holy Land. For those fortunate to be able to return, or who are in the country for an extended stay, it is strongly recommended that they consider visiting some of the Old Testament sites and some of the ancient Orthodox monasteries, such as the famous Monastery of Saint Catherine at Mount Sinai or the Monastery of Saint Saban near Bethlehem. Of course, the Western Wall of the Temple has religious significance for Christians in that the Temple worship is part of our shared spiritual heritage. Christians should not visit such places simply out of curiosity, but prayerfully.

A book worth bringing to all the holy places is John J. Kilgallen's *A New Testament Guide to the Holy Land*. This beautiful book is not a tourist guide but a book which relates each place to the New Testament passages, provides geographical and archeological background, and concludes each section with a profoundly spiritual meditation. Thus, it is a *spiritual* guide to the holy places. It could convert a frenetic tour into a pilgrimage. Equally valuable as a scriptural and meditative guide to the holy places is Stephen Doyle's *The Pilgrim's New Guide to the Holy Land*.

6.

The Holy Sepulchre
Like No Other Place On Earth

ATTITUDES TOWARDS THE HOLY SEPULCHRE

By definition, the empty tomb, or sepulchre, of Jesus Christ would have to be the most hallowed spot on earth for those who believe he was and is the unique Son of God and that he rose bodily from the dead at this spot, "ascended into heaven and sitteth at the right hand of the Father." This central tenet of Christianity has been memorialized for nearly seventeen hundred years by a succession of shrines over the very places of the cross and tomb. Jerusalem's earliest Christians kept the memory alive during the first centuries when Christian worship there was deliberately displaced by the erection of monuments to the gods of Rome.

The earliest Christian monument, built by Constantine and Helena in the early 300s, is said to have been extraordinarily impressive, second to none in the Roman world. It was called the Church of the Anastasis, the Greek word for Resurrection. After subsequent Persian and Arab desecrations and destructions, the Crusaders built a fine church over the ruins, but it could not have been of the original Byzantine magnificence. The nine hundred year old Crusader-built edifice has suffered from fires, neglect and lack of cooperation among the churches in restoration efforts. Nevertheless, it is like no other place on earth.

Critics love to ridicule the Church of the Holy Sepulchre, gloating over anecdotes about interchurch conflicts which, in truth, have occurred. A May 1995 article in *Atlantic Monthly* sums up the church in these unflattering terms:

> The Church of the Holy Sepulchre is partitioned among fractious sects—Greek Orthodox, Roman Catholic, Armenian Catholic, the Coptic Church, Ethiopian Orthodox, and Syrian Orthodox. The church is darkly beautiful and musty, almost rank. It is in an endless state of disrepair, with scaffolding everywhere, because the sects can rarely agree on how to proceed. If a building can be said to reveal the personality of its owner, then the Holy Sepulchre reveals Christianity to be quarrelsome, mysterious and alluring.

To correct the record, it should be noted that the Armenian community at the Holy Sepulchre is the Armenian Orthodox Church, not the much smaller Armenian Catholic Church. Also, as is pointed out in Chapter 12, a new spirit of cooperation among these ancient communities is very much in the air.

After describing the pristine beauty of the original Byzantine church on the site, Amos Elon, in *Jerusalem: City of Mirrors*, gives us this depressing description of the present structure:

> The smaller, more modest Crusader church we see today was built at about the same time as the cathedrals of Chartres and Vezelay. Columns and vaultings of this church have recently been cleaned or

reconstructed. In the process, some of the clean, medieval lines of the Crusader church have reemerged from the dark clutter that prevailed in most parts until 1975. But it still takes a lot of goodwill and imagination to conceive the original pristine beauty. The mean, imprisoned forecourt is still reached through a hole in the wall of the Arab street. The jumble of buildings and disconnected chapels, the maze of dark corridors and nondescript rooms, still make it a very ugly church, albeit historical. The Victorian-Greek 'improvements' of the nineteenth century—the almost invariably bad art, the unbelievably mediocre modern frescoes—disfigure the Holy Sepulchre even more. Few discerning visitors in the past two hundred years have had much good to say about it. It jumbles together, under one roof, Christ's alleged prison, Adam's tomb, the Pillar of Flagellation, 'Mount' Calvary, the Stone of Unction, Christ's sepulchre, and the Center of the Earth, as well as the site of the resurrected Christ's meeting with Mary Magdalene.

To the eye of the unbeliever the principal judgment may be that the place is an aesthetic disappointment, but a believer looks well beyond such superficial considerations. Most are truly overwhelmed by just being there. The building consists of numerous chapels representing various artistic styles, decorated in different centuries by artists from a variety of cultures. The first impression is confusion and disorientation.

The crowds move from chapel to chapel continuously. There is an atmosphere of great sadness surrounding the spot of the crucifixion. People express their sorrow in many ways. At the tomb some seem wary, not knowing what to expect when their turn comes to enter the small, confined burial room, passing by the Greek Orthodox lay brothers who guard it.

Some tourists, more curiosity seekers, walk around aimlessly, like the woman quoted by Father Wild, who, passing by Christ's tomb, asked her husband loudly, "What's that, George?" Then there was the pilgrim who asked his guide, in all seriousness: "Is there a body in the tomb?"

Possessing a wry sense of humor, the guide quipped: "If there is, Christianity is done for." This writer personally witnessed a group of people pushing and shoving and arguing loudly with the security officers in front of the tomb. They were angry because there would be a brief delay in their entry into Jesus' tomb while one of the frequent religious processions stopped there briefly to pray.

Even serious Western pilgrims, not knowing what to expect, are dumfounded by the maze of interconnected chapels, the proliferation of oil lamps and the proximity of the site of Calvary to the sepulchre. Much advance explanation is needed in the form of reading material and knowledgeable guides. Multilingual pamphlets should be available outside the church.

In contrast to the sarcasm, ridicule and petty complaints of some is the refreshing observation by Father Hoade, a Franciscan who spent many years in the Old City, writing in his *Guide to the Holy Land*:

> One must visit and revisit this sanctuary many a time; one must delay for long, and especially in the hours of solitude, in the hours of silence, when shades softly fall over the vast Basilica, and there remains under the darkened ceiling nothing of light save the flickering and mysterious light of lamps. Oh, the ineffable and unforgettable sweetness of the hours here passed, where was consummated the Divine Holocaust of love; here where the great ransom was paid whereby we were redeemed and saved; here in the temple of divine mercy where the agonizing Jesus prayed for His executioners, and to the penitent thief spoke the consoling words: 'This day thou shalt be with Me in Paradise.'

It is one of the most unfortunate aspects of current tours that most visitors make but one visit, often for less than an hour, to this place where they could profitably spend an entire week. Many must sense the inadequacy of their visit as their guide ushers them out to go to dinner. Pilgrims should try to go there every day while in Jerusalem, cutting out something else if need be. It is a place to linger, a time to cherish forever.

DESCRIPTION

While there are many more beautiful churches in the world, the Holy Sepulchre may be the most exotic, not to mention the most significant. With a little imagination and concentration, one can focus on "the bare rock of Calvary, supporting a Cross, and the rude rock of the Holy Sepulchre, where sits an Angel from Heaven on the stone that has been rolled back ...," to quote Father Hoade.

The courtyard and entrance way are not at all pretentious, since the church is located in the very midst of the teeming Old City. It stands cheek to jowl with other buildings on nearly every side, even an historic mosque dating to the Muslim conquest in the 600s. Near the entrance is a Greek Orthodox convent. The Anglican Church has the use of a chapel in the upper part of the convent, courtesy of the Greek Patriarch. Next to it is the Armenian Chapel of Saint John. Beside it is the Coptic Chapel of Saint Michael, from which there is access to the humble habitations of the Ethiopian Church on the roof. That this impoverished African church has been able to maintain a monastery here, albeit on the roof of the building, is a poignant reminder of the diversity of the Christian religion. Likewise, the historic "rights" of the ancient Coptic, or Egyptian, Church testify to our rich variety.

Since shortly after the end of the Crusades, two Muslim families have had control of the door to the church. One keeps the key; the other has the right to open it. For hundreds of years the church was permitted by the Turkish government to be opened only for major holy days, and Christians had to pay an entrance fee.

The ritual for a solemn opening of the door is hard to believe. One of the communities having "rights" in the church knocks at the wicket. A Greek sacristan calls the Muslim porter, who hands out a ladder, which is used to reach the door lock. Three bells announce the opening, one for each of the three "major" communities (Orthodox, Armenian and Catholic), all of whom must agree.

The first major site encountered after entering the church is the so-called Stone of Unction, or Stone of the Anointing, commemorating the anointing of the body of Jesus after he was taken down from the cross. Although this may or may not be the precise spot of the anointing of his body by the holy women, it must be quite close by, and it is the traditional spot to meditate on this event. The stone "belongs" to the Greek Orthodox, Catholics, Armenians and Copts. Nearby are living quarters for Armenian and Coptic clergy.

From there one may enter the rotunda, in the center of which is the sepulchre itself. The little edifice over the burial place, called an "edicule," is about thirty feet by twenty feet. The facade is ornate in the extreme, including oil lamps and representations of the resurrection.

There is usually a line of people waiting to enter the edicule. Inside are two compartments, the first a sort of vestibule which can hold two or three people. It is called the Chapel of the Angel and would be the approximate place where the angel announced to the women, "He has risen."

A four-foot high passage requires one to bow down in order to enter the room of the Holy Sepulchre itself, which is only six feet by six feet. Three worshippers can comfortably kneel before the tomb at one time. A marble slab marks the burial place and covers the natural rock beneath. For those pilgrims who have prepared themselves, these brief minutes inside the edicule, in the words of Father Hoade:

> ... leave an indelible and sweet record on the soul of one whose lot

it may be to cross the threshold of that mortuary chamber which held the body of the Crucified, and to kiss that sacred stone on which the hands of Joseph of Arimathaea and Nicodemus piously laid the remains of their beloved Master. If he should live a thousand years, he shall never forget—to forget would be impossible—the day, the hour, the fleeting moment in which he visited the 'Glorious Sepulchre' of God made man.

Greek, Armenian and Latin Masses are celebrated each day at the sepulchre.

Behind the edicule is a chapel maintained today by the Copts. It is at the other end of the Holy Sepulchre. Pilgrims may enter this tiny chapel and kiss the rock formation, presumably also part of the tomb of Christ. A solitary Coptic priest holds vigil inside the entrance. There is room for but one person at a time to enter and kneel to pray. There is something sweet about the simplicity, even poverty, of this little chapel and its guardians.

Nearby in the church are the Chapel of the Syrian Jacobites, the Magdalene Chapel, the Franciscan Church of the Apparition, the Franciscan convent, the Greek Chapel of Saint Longinus (the soldier who pierced Jesus' side), the Armenian Chapel of Saint Helen, the Latin Chapel of the Finding of the Cross and the Greek Chapel of the Mocking.

Finally we come to a rather steep staircase leading up to the higher elevation of the crucifixion site, Calvary. The area consists of two small chapels divided by monumental pillars. To the right is a chapel maintained by Catholics, covered in marble and mosaics of Jesus being nailed to the cross, the holy women watching the crucifixion, and Abraham preparing to sacrifice his son Isaac.

The other chapel is Greek Orthodox. Its altar is directly over the exposed rocky outcropping where, according to the oldest tradition, the cross stood. Fervent pilgrims wait their turn to kneel and bend down to kiss the spot. Beneath Calvary is a place called the Chapel of Adam, commemorating what can be no more than a pious legend, that Adam was here buried and that on the day of the crucifixion the saving blood of the Savior fell upon Adam's head.

Close by the Holy Sepulchre stands the Church of the Redeemer, a major center of Lutheran worship. The church is a reconstruction of a Crusader church which, in turn, replaced one built at the time of Charlemagne, about 800 A.D. Being within yards of Calvary and the empty tomb, it is a very meaningful place for services by church communities not having the privilege of holding formal services inside the Holy Sepulchre Church itself.

AUTHENTICITY

The main reason for skepticism about the authenticity of the traditional sites of Calvary and the Holy Sepulchre is their location *within* the walls of the Old City. All indications from the gospels, not to mention ancient Hebrew regulations, would indicate the crucifixion and burial must have taken place *outside* the city walls. This objection, however, is no longer defensible, as we know the walls were extended outward a few years after the crucifixion. The other causes of natural skepticism are the unexpected closeness of the tomb to the place of crucifixion, and the fact that "Mount" Calvary is no more than a knoll.

Father Hoade quotes from Saint Jerome, the great Bible translator, writing in 395 A.D.:

> From Hadrian's time until the reign of Constantine, for about a hundred eighty years, the Gentiles used to worship an image of Jupiter set up in the place of the resurrection and on the rock of the cross a marble statue of Venus. For the authors of the persecution supposed

that by polluting the Holy Places with idols they would do away with our faith in the resurrection and the cross.

Father Hoade tells us that in 44 A.D., about fourteen years after the crucifixion, King Agrippa extended the city walls beyond Golgotha, or Calvary, following north more or less to the line of the present wall. The wall erected by Emperor Hadrian a century later followed the line of Agrippa's wall, as does the present wall built by the Turks.

John 19:20 notes that Calvary was outside the wall in 30 A.D., but "near the city." There was a garden there containing a new tomb, and the tomb was "close by." (John 19:42.) Today we cannot see Calvary and the tomb as they were in 30 A.D., but archeology gives us a good idea of the topography. The gospel writers call the site, in Aramaic, Golgotha. In Greek that becomes Kranion, in English Cranium or skull. The Latin translation is Calvary, a bald scalp. The word "mount" as in "Mount Calvary" does not appear in any of the gospels. It is referred to as a "place" called Calvary (or Golgotha). Some have speculated that the term skull place was a reference to the skull of Adam being buried there, Jesus being the "Second Adam." Or possibly a rocky outcropping in the form of a skull. The reference to the place as a "mount" did not occur until the fourth century A.D., after the surrounding rock formations had been excavated for the construction of the basilica, leaving the rocky spot surrounding the crucifixion an isolated knoll some fifteen feet above its surroundings.

Interestingly, it fits very nicely that the place of burial would be right outside the city walls as they existed before Agrippa's extension. Even today, outside the eastern wall, facing the Mount of Olives, there are sprawling Jewish and Muslim cemeteries from antiquity. Fittingly, the edicule which surmounts Jesus' tomb today is in the form of

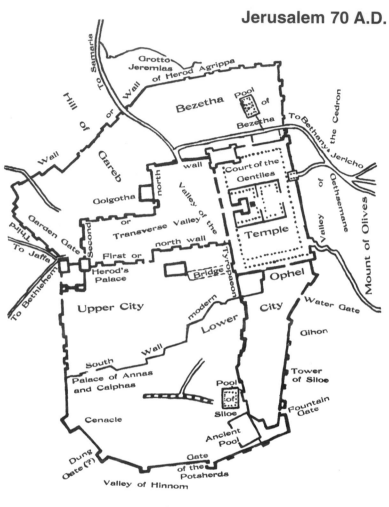

Herod Agrippa's extension of the city wall after the crucifixion.

ancient Jewish tombs, composed of two chambers, the first a vestibule for mourning, the second containing a couch cut into the rock, on which the body was laid.

As Father Hoade notes, the exact place of Jesus' crucifixion and

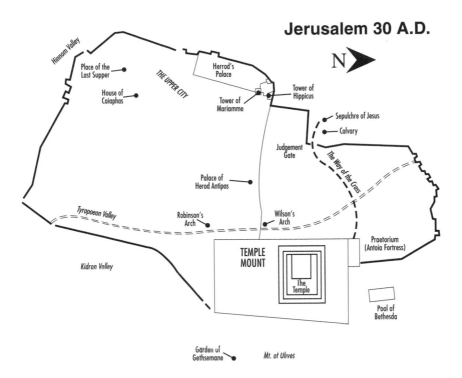

City walls at the time of Jesus' crucifixion.

resurrection would have been sacred to the infant church as it is described in the Acts of the Apostles. "It would be absurd to think that the early Christians of Jerusalem, and conversions came in thousands, were not interested in the place connected with the life and death of Christ." The statue of Jupiter and altar to Venus, intended no doubt to obscure the memory, served to mark the site until Constantine's time.

In 335 Constantine's engineers removed the pagan shrines and platform, exposing the original site. The fourth century historian Eusebius says this discovery was "beyond all hope," since Christians had feared the Romans had destroyed the tomb before building the platform and pagan shrines over it.

Constantine's great basilica was destroyed in 614 during a rapacious Persian raid, but was soon rebuilt by Abbot Modestus. It was unharmed by the Muslim Conquest of 636 but destroyed again in 1009 by the mad Caliph al-Hakim. It was rebuilt again in 1048 by the Byzantine Emperor Constantine Monomachus with permission of the Muslims. About 1100, right after their conquest of the city, the Crusaders erected the present structure, which, in the words of Father Hoade: "Although despoiled of its early splendor and disfigured by later additions and deplorable restoration, exists to this day in main outline."

Father Hoade's assessment of the authenticity of the Holy Sepulchre is confirmed by the comments of the two English authors of *Every Pilgrim's Guide to the Holy Land*. Norman Wareham and Jill Gill write as Anglicans. Their church originally supported the authenticity of the Garden Tomb but has withdrawn its support of that claim. Regarding the fact that the Holy Sepulchre is inside the present city walls, they say:

> For those familiar with the Gospel story and the words of Mrs. C.F. Alexander's famous hymn recalling the green hill outside the City walls, it is bewildering to discover that the Church of the Holy Sepulchre is today almost in the centre of the Old City. Scripture clearly records that Christ suffered 'outside the gate' and in a place called Golgotha (the place of the Skull) adjoining which was a garden. It is hardly surprising therefore that some Christians find the Garden Tomb, situated a few hundred metres outside the Damascus Gate, more in keeping with their expectations. Nevertheless the hypothesis is very strong in support of the claim that the ground on which the Church stands was in fact outside the City walls at the time of the crucifixion.

It is important to appreciate that in Our Lord's lifetime the northern wall of Jerusalem ran roughly from Herod's Palace (where the Citadel now stands) to the Fortress of Antonia. Indeed, one of the purposes of this great stronghold was to defend the City from the north. Golgotha was then *outside* this wall. However, the historian Flavius Josephus records that in the middle of the first century, some time after the Crucifixion, Jerusalem began to spread northwards and a suburb developed. This new area required protection so two other walls were subsequently built.

It was not until AD 135 when the Roman Emperor Hadrian completely redesigned the City, that the northern wall was constructed in its final position. The lower courses of this Roman structure can still be seen below the Damascus Gate. Thus the Church of the Holy Sepulchre is now well within the confines of the Old City and (its site) has been for over eighteen hundred years.

Wareham and Gill argue convincingly, as follows:

Inside the Church of the Holy Sepulchre and within a few metres of the site of Our Lord's Tomb are, hewn out of the bedrock, two complete first century Jewish tombs. This proves that the area was outside the walls in Our Lord's time because burials never took place within the City confines as the ground was thus rendered unclean.

It is probable that there were other tombs in the area and that the rocky mound of Calvary was chosen for crucifixions simply because it could be seen from the walls and acted as a reminder of the consequences of breaking the law.

During the four decades after the Resurrection, the followers of Jesus would undoubtedly have known the precise location of Calvary and the Tomb. Many of them had been first hand witnesses to the aftermath of this momentous event—not least among them were Mary Magdalene, Mary the mother of James, Peter and the other disciples who hurried to the Sepulchre on the first Easter morning. Indeed, the Tomb itself most probably remained in Christian hands because it belonged to Joseph of Arimathea who was a follower of Jesus.

It is important to bear in mind that at this stage these early Christians anticipated that Jesus would return in their own lifetimes. They did not then appreciate the significance of His promise that He would 'be with them always'—in the unseen presence of the Holy Spirit. It was not necessary therefore to physically mark the Tomb for future generations to identify, but is surely reasonable to assume that the site was venerated by His early followers. They in turn must have passed on very accurate and reliable information as to its exact location. This was the beginning of the 'oral tradition' and it was extremely strong.

In AD 70 the Roman Emperor Titus sacked the City. Herod's magnificent Temple, the centre of Jewish worship and culture, was totally destroyed together with all other buildings of significance. Indeed Jesus Himself predicted that 'not one stone would be left upon another.' However it seems most likely that Calvary and the Tomb would have escaped the attention of Titus's troops, being already waste ground, an 'unclean' burial place, with no buildings erected upon it.

There then followed a very sad period of Jerusalem's history when the city lay in ruins, rather like some of those in Europe after the Second World War. However, domestic life gradually began to return to some degree of normality as the inhabitants had not been banished, although many of the Jewish leaders were slain. Thus the seeds of the early Church were able to survive.

According to Wareham and Gill the rest of the story concerning the site of Calvary and the Tomb is as follows:

In AD 135, sixty-five years after the sacking of the City by Titus, the Jews were finally banished by Hadrian who totally rebuilt Jerusalem in the form of a typical Roman colonial town renamed 'Aelia Capitolina.' He constructed a large podium over the entire area of Calvary and the Tomb upon which were erected in honour of the Roman gods a statue of Jupiter and a Temple to Venus. Saint Jerome suggests that Hadrian did this in order to obscure the sites and prevent the Christians from venerating them. Whether this is true or not the fact remains that his action marked their position for future generations to uncover.

Although Hadrian had banished the Jews, the Gentile Church of Graeco-Roman origin nevertheless continued. There is an extant record of all the Graeco-Roman Bishops and Eusebius, who was Bishop of Caesarea from AD 313, mentions that the Gentile Church in Jerusalem flourished.

Early in the fourth century the Roman Emperor Constantine was converted to Christianity. Macarius, the Bishop of Jerusalem at that time, assured him that Calvary and the Tomb were to be found beneath the Temple to Venus and the statue of Jupiter. Constantine expressed a desire to 'make that most blessed spot, the place of the Resurrection, visible to all and given over to veneration.'

Consequently in AD 325 work started on demolishing the Temple and removing the podium. The whole area when cleared revealed the small mound of Calvary, while a little to the west rose the rockface containing the Sepulchre. In a letter which Constantine wrote to Bishop Macarius he said: 'No words can express how good the Saviour has been to us ... that the monument of His Holy Passion, hidden for so many years, has now at last been restored to the faithful and set free..."

The archeological and historical evidence of authenticity of the site of Calvary and the Tomb of Jesus Christ within the present-day Church of the Holy Sepulchre is strong enough to resolve any reasonable doubt.

7.

Being in Jerusalem
Awesome And Overwhelming

Endless volumes have been written about the Holy City, and its fascinations merit such attention. The walled Old City, a square mile of history within the sprawling modern city, was all that there was until a century ago. Therefore, it will be the focus of this chapter. Nevertheless, one arriving in Jerusalem will spend considerable time traveling around the modern city outside the walls. This turbulent city of several hundred thousand souls requires some introduction, to put it mildly.

WEST AND EAST JERUSALEM

Most travelers today approach Jerusalem on the road from Ben Gurion Airport outside Tel Aviv. The road rises from the coastal plain to the aridly beautiful hills of Judea. Jerusalem sprawls over the hill-

The Walled Old City, from the Mount of Olives. Dome of the Rock to left. Ancient cemeteries outside the wall.

sides, covering many square miles. Arriving from the coast, one first encounters West Jerusalem, comprising about two-thirds of the city. This is Jewish territory, as is obvious from the Western dress of the people on the streets. Passing Mount Herzl, where the martyred President Rabin is laid to rest, and Mea Shearim, an ultra-Orthodox section, one finally arrives at the Damascus Gate.

West Jerusalem, the thriving Jewish side of town, has been part of Israel since the new nation's beginning in 1948. The Old City and East Jerusalem, the Arab side of town, were ruled by Jordan until Israel captured them, along with the West Bank, Gaza Strip, Sinai Desert and Golan Heights in the Six Day War of 1967. Giving back any of these territories to the Arabs has been a most painful prospect to consider for Israelis since that time. Still, I have it on a very good source that the majority would willingly exchange land for a secure peace.

If one has the opportunity, there are places of great interest within the modern city, including Mount Herzl, Yad Vashem (the Holocaust Museum), the two campuses of the great Hebrew University, Mount Scopus, the Knesset (Parliament), the Israel Museum, the cosmopolitan pedestrian malls near the Old City, the famous King David Hotel, the Shrine of the Book, the newly-excavated City of David, and the Holy Land Hotel's model of the Jerusalem of Jesus' time. Need I say more! Several of these sites are on Christian tour itineraries. All are more than worth a visit, but that would necessitate a return trip, a prospect seriously worth considering.

East Jerusalem is like another city, traditionally occupied by Arabs but with a burgeoning population of Jewish settlers now. It is primarily a Muslim city, although several thousand native Palestinian Christians still live among the Muslims. The language on the street is Arabic rather than Hebrew, except in the new settlements. Arab headdress has become more and more common on men, and more and more women have returned to traditional Muslim dress.

Unemployment here is extremely high. Resentment of Israel is higher yet. Jews generally do not feel comfortable in East Jerusalem, and many would not set foot on its territory or on the West Bank. Hopefully this mutual distrust will someday be a not-so-fond memory.

Nevertheless the opportunity for a Westerner to "get lost" walking in an Arab city will appeal to the more adventurous. The same may be said of the ultra-Orthodox Jewish neighborhoods like Mea Shearim, where one enters on the Sabbath at the risk of being stoned, if immodestly clad. Special attractions in the East Jerusalem area include the

Mount of Olives, the ancient cemeteries surrounding the Old City, Mount Zion (including the Dormition Abbey and Cenacle), the Tombs of David and Absolom, and the Garden Tomb.

Jerusalem the Holy

At this point it is recommended that the reader open the Bible to Psalm 122 to set the mood for what follows. This Psalm of longing to be in Jerusalem was recited by pilgrims of old as they approached the city. It is a prayer seeking peace, health and prosperity for the city and its people. "Pray for the peace of Jerusalem." Because this city has been, of old, the special earthly abode of the Lord, one should approach it with reverence and awe. A few moments of silent meditation would be appropriate.

Kissing the ground is a tradition here when one arrives at one's destination. For Christians there is the awareness that Jesus Christ walked all over this ground, making it forever sacred. We say about a lover: "He worshiped the ground she walked on." This figure of speech evokes the sentiment we may properly feel here. It is the city of the kings, the prophets, God's chosen people and, finally, the city where our human race was once and for all reconciled with God. It is more than brick and mortar and people. It is a state of mind. It is something unearthly. From here Jesus ascended to the Father and sent us the Spirit. Here, it is said, he will return on the Day of Judgment.

It is the very heart of Jewishness, where the Ark of the Covenant once rested behind a curtain in the Holy of Holies within the Temple. For Muslims it is always called El Quds, "The Holy," because of its close association with the patriarchs, with Jesus and with Mohammed who, according to the Koran, ascended to heaven from the Temple Mount. They also believe the Last Judgment will take place here. For

Christians it is, preeminently, the place where the blood of the Redeemer saved the world.

GETTING AROUND

The Old City has been walled for most of its history, but the walls have periodically been destroyed and rebuilt. Most of the impressive system of stone walls we see today were built between 1537 and 1541 at the zenith of Ottoman culture and power by Turkish Sultan Suleiman the Magnificent, so they are nearly five hundred years old. Parts, however, were built by Herod the Great, just before the birth of Christ. There is a walkway along the greater part of the walls, from which one may appreciate the surrounding city, the Judean hills, the Kidron Valley and the Mount of Olives. While this is a popular pastime, the reader is cautioned about walking in isolated stretches alone.

There are eight gates to the Old City, most having histories going back many centuries. They are as follows: Herod's Gate, Damascus Gate, New Gate, Jaffa Gate, Zion Gate, Dung Gate, Golden (or Beautiful) Gate (which is walled off) and Saint Stephen's (or Lion) Gate, in counterclockwise order starting from the north. Some names will ring a bell with those familiar with the Bible.

Jews and Christians share a tradition that the Messiah will enter the city through the Golden Gate when he comes. Apparently fearing the Jewish or Christian Messiah might do just that, a cautious Muslim ruler, hedging his bets, bricked in the Golden Gate during the Middle Ages in order to keep the Messiah out! The Golden Gate remains walled up today.

Damascus Gate is a principal entrance to the Old City from East Jerusalem. The area outside the gate is usually crowded with Palestinians, and is of considerable interest to curious Westerners.

Jaffa Gate is the main entrance to the Christian Quarter. Many shops cater to Christians, and the patriarchal churches of the various Christian communities are nearby. Pilgrims arriving alone will be most at ease if they enter the Old City through this gate. Zion Gate is the entrance way to the Jewish Quarter and the Armenian Quarter, while the Dung Gate also leads to the Jewish Quarter and the Temple Mount area.

Inside the gates you are at once in a medieval maze of narrow lanes. Getting lost, unless you are with a guide, is inevitable. If you return to the Old City to explore it on your own, you will constantly be turned around. Do not let this discourage you, as every lane is well worth following, and you cannot go very far without coming to a landmark or gate.

THE QUARTERS

The Christian Quarter contains the great Church (or Basilica) of the Holy Sepulchre, the Lutheran Church of the Redeemer, the headquarters and printing press of the Franciscan Order, the patriarchal offices and churches of the Latin (Roman Catholic) Patriarchate, the Greek Orthodox Patriarchate, and the Greek Catholic (Melkite) Patriarchal Vicar. There are also a few church-operated hospices, including Casa Nova, the Greek Catholic Foyer, Notre Dame Center (just outside New Gate), an Evangelical drop-in center and hospice (just inside Jaffa Gate) and a hospice at the Greek Orthodox Patriarchate.

The Armenian Quarter is between the Christian and Jewish Quarters. The Armenians were the first nation to adopt Christianity *en masse*, and they have had a continuous presence in Jerusalem since very early times. Their quarter is usually quiet, and their exquisite Cathedral of Saint James is open to the public only for a brief period each afternoon. The church stands on the spot where, according to tradition, the Apostle

James was martyred several years after the crucifixion, as reported in the Acts of the Apostles, Chapter 12. The quarter has the architectural ambiance of a fortress, no doubt owing to its history of needing to defend itself from marauders. The memory of the Armenian Holocaust at the hands of the Turks between 1915 and 1923, when over a million people were killed or starved, is kept alive in a museum in the quarter. These proud people lost a major percentage of their worldwide numbers and are determined not to let the world forget. Maronite, Anglican and Syrian Orthodox churches of historic significance can also be found in the Armenian Quarter.

Since the 600s the Temple Mount, holiest of places to Jews, has been occupied by two of the world's most important Muslim holy places, Al Aksa Mosque and the gorgeous Dome of the Rock. The Temple Mount is known to Muslims as the Haram al-Sharif, which means Noble Sanctuary. The Jews, deprived of the use of the site, must content themselves with doing what they have done for nineteen hundred years, pray at the Western Wall, all that remains of the Temple's embankment. Note that it is no longer called the Wailing Wall. Since the Jewish takeover of the area as a result of the 1967 War, it is a much happier place, no more a place for weeping and wailing. Israel continues to excavate beneath the Temple Mount, causing alarm and consternation to pious Muslims.

The Jewish Quarter and Muslim Quarter both border on the Temple Mount (Haram Al-Sharif) and are a study in contrasts. While the Muslim Quarter is teeming with Arabs shopping in their bazaars, and appears to be decaying in its infrastructure, the Jewish Quarter, rebuilt since 1967, is a modernistic oasis in the Old City. Between 1948 and 1967 the Jordanians had destroyed much of the medieval Jewish Quarter, or ghetto, including ancient Sephardic synagogues, so Israel, after capturing the Old City in 1967, took the opportunity to build something radically new—but still very Jewish. The little shopping plazas are sophisticated. Zionism is promoted in store windows. It is well lit and safe. An ancient Roman street, known as the Cardo, is being excavated, and a visitor may see the restoration of ruined synagogues and other evidences of Jewish life of medieval times. The religious climate is ultra-Orthodox, and it is said that nonobservant Jews feel less than welcome. Nevertheless, it is highly recommended that Christian pilgrims tour the quarter. Some tours make it a point to visit the old synagogues as a gesture of interfaith friendship and a recognition of Christian roots in Judaism.

Apart from worshipping at the Holy Sepulchre and Calvary, the most prominent Christian activity in the Old City (shopping in the bazaars aside!) is making the Way of the Cross on the Via Dolorosa. This most moving devotion began during the first Christian period (300-600 A.D.) under Byzantine rule, and took its present shape during the Crusades. It will be described more fully in the chapter on preparing for your pilgrimage. Not to be missed is the Friday afternoon tradition in which hundreds of pilgrims follow Jesus' route through the city on the way to his crucifixion. The Church of the Holy Sepulchre, as a result, tends to be crowded on Friday afternoons.

The Old City grows on you the more you walk its narrow cobblestone streets. Something strange and unexpected awaits you around every corner. From early morning to dusk it is always an intriguing blend of sights and sounds and people of different countries and faiths, all going about their business. Church bells ring, muezzins call the faithful to prayer, merchants try to entice customers into their shops, monks and rabbinical students and Muslim holy men pass one another, all seeming to be in a hurry to get somewhere.

The Hebrew and Arabic and English street signs point to places steeped in the history of the City. Over a cup of Arabic or Armenian coffee one can relax and watch the parade go by and enjoy being a part of the scene for a little while.

8.

Jewish and Muslim
Holy Places
Our Common Heritage

INTEREST IN EACH OTHER'S HOLY PLACES

The travel agenda for Jews and Christians differs a great deal, as Jews do not consider Jesus to be the Messiah, Redeemer and Son of God. On the other hand, Christians have every reason to visit the multitude of places sacred to Jews, as we understand our religion to be the fulfillment of God's covenant with the people of Israel and its extension to the whole human race.

Muslims respect the patriarchs of the Hebrew Scriptures, as well as Jesus. They see their religion as the fulfillment of all of the revelations from Abraham to Mohammed, including the revelation to the "prophet" Jesus. They have a special devotion to Mary, the Mother of Jesus. Christians and Jews, on the other hand, have no devotional reason to visit Muslim shrines. Doing so as an expression of respect and good will, however, is a gesture of friendship which is appreciated by many Muslims. Many mosques are places of great serenity and beauty. Additionally, we share with the Muslims the understanding of God, "Allah" in Arabic, as the one all-holy, just, wise and kind creator of the world, the God of Abraham, of Moses and of Jesus. It is imperative that Christians come to better understand the religious life and ethical values of the Muslims, if there is to be peace in the next century. As pilgrims in the Holy Land we have that opportunity.

MUSLIM HOLY PLACES

In the Holy Land the Muslim places of greatest interest are situated on the Temple Mount (Haram al-Sharif). The entire area is sacred to Islam and claimed by Muslims. While the great mosque building known as Al-Aksa and the gorgeous Dome of the Rock cover only a small portion of the Temple Mount, the entire area is deemed a "mosque" by the Islamic Wakf Administration.

Al-Aksa is a place of Friday worship, while the Dome of the Rock is really a shrine, a place for quiet prayer. Al-Aksa contains fabulous oriental carpets by the hundreds, a pleasant walking surface for the mandatory shoeless feet. Both buildings were completed during the first century of Islam, over thirteen hundred years ago. Non-Muslims enter only at certain times, and are expected to show great respect. The Haram Al-Sharif is the holiest mosque in Islam, apart from the two great mosques in Saudi Arabia at Mecca and Medina, and is surely deserving of our respect and interest.

The large, uncut rocky outcropping inside the Dome of the Rock is considered by tradition to be the top of Mount Moriah, the place where Abraham, in obedience to God, prepared to sacrifice his only son, Isaac. The innocent son, carrying the wood which was to be used

The Al-Aksa Mosque in Jerusalem. The city is known in the Muslim World as "El-Quds," or "The Holy."

in his sacrifice, inquired where the sacrificial lamb was. This beautiful and poignant story of faith and trust in God appears in the twenty-second chapter of Genesis, which might profitably be read *before* entering the Dome of the Rock. To Christians this story beautifully prefigures the sacrifice of the Lamb of God on Calvary. (Of course, no organized Christian prayer or worship service would be permitted at this place.) The Dome of the Rock is truly a holy place for us as well as for Jews and Muslims, because of its location. Fortunately, it is on most tourist itineraries. Unfortunately many Christians do not, while there, contemplate that they are at the traditional site of Abraham's act of faith and of the Temple of Solomon, as well as the Second Temple where Jesus taught and prayed.

For Muslims this area has special importance as the focal point of the Prophet Mohammed's Night Journey. About 620 A.D., according to Islamic teaching, Mohammed fell asleep one night in Mecca and was awakened by the angel Gabriel, who took him to al-Buraq, a winged horse. Gabriel and Mohammed, according to the Koran, sped on al-Buraq to Jerusalem, to the "furthest mosque." Mohammed then dismounted and prayed at the holy Rock, where he was joined in prayer by Abraham, Moses, Jesus and other prophets. From there they were taken up to heaven, and the Prophet, according to the Koran, received the command to pray five times a day, as well as a major revelation concerning the religion of Islam. While Christians do not share these beliefs, we should endeavor to understand them so we can better appreciate those whose lives revolve around them.

THE WESTERN WALL

All Christian pilgrims visit the Western Wall, formerly known as the Wailing Wall, which is in actuality part of the foundation of the Temple Mount, rather than a remnant of the temple building itself. Nevertheless, it is extremely impressive and historic. Its sacredness is often overlooked by Christian visitors, who go there more out of curiosity to watch the black-clothed Orthodox Jews at prayer.

Their prayer practices are indeed moving, and worth observing, but hopefully more and more Christian visitors to the Wall area will see it as holy to us too. To remind yourself of the continuity of worship of our one true God at this site for three thousand years, read aloud with your group Solomon's prayer to the Lord God at the dedication of the temple. (First Kings 8:22-30, 33-53, 56-61.) Having done so will make you feel a kinship with the pious Jewish worshippers in your midst. This is another place at which to linger, or, if possible, return alone. In addition to the frequent bar and bat mitzvahs (ceremonies for Jewish sons and daughters coming of age spiritually) there are numerous Orthodox Jewish men, fully bearded and all in black, reading and praying from the Torah, bowing their heads and repeatedly touching the Wall. Cracks in the Wall are always full of slips of paper containing prayer requests, even some faxed from the United States!

OTHER BIBLICAL SITES

The city of Hebron, about twenty-five miles south of Jerusalem, is the site of the oldest shrine to believe in God as we know him; i.e., one, holy and loving of his people. This is the Cave of Machpelah, the burial place of the Patriarchs Abraham, Isaac and Jacob, as well as their wives Sarah, Rebecca and Leah. (As noted elsewhere, Rachel is buried just outside Bethlehem.) It is hard to overstate its spiritual significance, not only to Jews but to Muslims as well, who also claim the patriarchs as their spiritual fathers in faith. We Christians, if we consider the relationship of the Old Covenant to our understanding of its fulfillment in Jesus, will also want to worship the Lord God at this place. As of this writing, it is not on many itineraries because of the tension between Jewish settlers and Palestinians concerning control of the city and the great mosque (and synagogue) built over the ancient tombs. We can pray that this will change for the better soon. The loss of visitors has damaged the already marginal economy of Hebron. Christians should press for the inclusion of Hebron in itineraries as soon as possible.

Jacob's Well in Samaria is another place of biblical interest to Christians because of the story of the Samaritan woman at the well. It is off the beaten track, but there is a Greek Orthodox chapel. (Samaria is the region between Judea and Galilee.) Rachel's Tomb, on the edge of Bethlehem, deserves a brief stop for prayer and a reading of the Genesis passage concerning Jacob's burial of his wife there.

Mount Sinai, where Moses received the Ten Commandments, and Mount Nebo, where he died after gazing across the Jordan into the Promised Land, are both far out in the desert and usually not on Christian itineraries. One is in Egyptian territory, the other in Jordan. The intrepid will find plenty of inspiration here, and ancient monasteries may be visited. There is talk of a great pilgrimage to Mount Sinai in the year 2000 A.D. in commemoration of the turn of the millennium of Jesus' birth. Jericho, where the People of Israel crossed the River Jordan and defeated the Caananites in battle, has both Christian and Jewish holy memories, and is also worth a visit.

The Tombs of King David and his son Absalom are to be found just outside the Old City; David's on Mount Zion, Absalom's in an ancient cemetery. Both are disputed as to authenticity, but are, nevertheless, appropriate places for a reading of the relevant chapters in the books of Samuel. The so-called Tower of David, part of the Citadel complex inside the Jaffa Gate, merits a visit for the multimedia presentation on the City of Jerusalem, although the Tower was erected long after David's time. The Citadel, on the other hand, was constructed by the great builder, and greater scoundrel, known to us as King Herod.

Excavation of biblical sites from Hebrew times goes on constantly. The original City of David is one such in Jerusalem, a large area abutting Mount Zion. In Galilee a fishing vessel from Jesus' time has been rescued intact from the muck under the Sea of Galilee, and is on public display.

OTHER PLACES SACRED TO JEWS

Old synagogues, some in Jerusalem, are treasured by the Israeli people. These have been excavated and restored. Qumran, where the Dead

*One of the caves at Qumran along the Dead Sea, where the Dead Sea
Scrolls were found by an Arab shepherd boy in the late 1940s.*

Sea Scrolls were found in caves, is visited by curious Christian groups,
but generally with little sense of connection to our religion. In addition
to being a day of adventure in the desert, it should be reflected upon
that here were stored for safekeeping, around the time of Christ, many
precious scrolls of the scriptures, God' word. Why they were stored and
by whom is the subject of scholarly debate. These ancient scrolls may
now be viewed and studied at the Shrine of the Book, a major Israeli
attraction in Jerusalem. They include some of the oldest existing frag-
mentary texts of the Hebrew scriptures.

Two final Jewish holy places, not to be missed, are Masada and the
Holocaust Museum. Masada is the mountaintop retreat where the
Zealots, after an uprising in Jerusalem, held out for three years against

vastly superior forces and a prolonged Roman siege between 66 and 72 A.D. Masada is not biblical, but it is a sacred chapter in Jewish history. A visit by cable car to the top, overlooking the Dead Sea and the desert, moves every visitor very deeply. That also may be said of the Holocaust Museum, which should be a must on the Christian travel agenda. It is a sensitizing experience and forces those of us who claim the name Christian to come face to face with the genocide in which so many "Christians" were accomplices. It is a humbling experience and, hopefully, a learning experience we can take home with us.

Part Three

LIFE IN THE HOLY LAND TODAY

9

Christian Communities
In The Holy Land
Endangered Species

S peaking of the half-million Christians from around the world who yearly visit the Holy Land as pilgrims, Robert L. Wilkin, in *The Land Called Holy*, observes:

> Though in other ways they may be well-informed about the Middle East, few realize that Christianity's role in the land of the Bible is not restricted to the time of Jesus and Christian origins. The Christian religion has a long history in Palestine, the history of indigenous communities whose fortunes have been linked to the many conquerors—Romans, Arabs, Crusaders, Turks and Jews—and of national communities from other parts of the world, Copts from Egypt, Armenians, Syrians, Ethiopians, Russians, some of which have uninterrupted histories from antiquity to the present.

A writer in the 1995 Diocesan Bulletin of the Latin Patriarchate of Jerusalem speaks eloquently of those "who live where Jesus lived, around the holy places, who are the descendants of the very first ancient church which gave birth to all other churches."

The bulletin writer, Father Anton, sees the local Palestinian church like this:

> This church was born in Palestine together with Christ; it became a majority and then, beset by misfortune, dwindled to a minority again. Gradually reduced through the centuries, it became scarcely more than embers in the ashes until it was rekindled in the last century to become what it is today: the remarkable Church of the Holy Places.

And indeed, who cannot feel empathy for this small Christian community, or group of communities, and want to help them? Consider what they have been through in order to survive since the seventh century Muslim Conquest, as summarized by Wilken:

> Most were natives and had no other country to go to, and many, at least initially, did not convert to the faith of their new masters. In time they learned to pray in Arabic, translated the Scriptures into Arabic, and produced devotional and theological literature in the language of their conquerors. The Arabic-speaking Christians who live today in Israel, the West Bank, and Jordan are their descendants and hence the descendants of the first Christians. They are, as it were, the only indigenous Christian community in the world.

The forms of Christianity found in Jerusalem today are as varied as anywhere. In addition to Greek, Latin and Armenian patriarchs, there are in residence the titular heads of thirty-two other separate Christian communities.

CHURCH MEMBERSHIP

There are about one hundred and sixty-five thousand native Christians in the Holy Land, according to Thomas F. Stransky, rector of

The Cave of the Nativity in Bethlehem, traditional place of the birth of Christ. The oldest church in the world stands over the spot.

the Tantur Ecumenical Institute for Theological Studies in Jerusalem, writing in *America* magazine. In addition to the three largest communities (Greek Catholics, Greek Orthodox, and Roman Catholics), there are several thousand Maronite Catholics and smaller numbers of Syrian Orthodox, Armenian Orthodox, Coptic Orthodox, Ethiopian Orthodox, Armenian Catholics, and Syrian Catholics. Among Protestant communities, there are about two thousand Anglicans, one thousand Lutherans, and lesser numbers of members of other churches, including Evangelical churches and missions. Christians are concentrated in Jerusalem, Bethlehem and its environs, Ramallah, Nazareth, Haifa and in numerous small towns in Galilee (Northern Israel).

Statistics on church membership in the Holy Land are somewhat questionable and difficult to verify. Attrition due to emigration continues. Numbers of native Christians in the Holy Land have ebbed and flowed over the centuries, as have the fortunes of particular church communities. It is estimated that 650,000 Christians of Palestinian origin live in the diaspora, mostly in the Americas and Western Europe. That is several times the number remaining in the cradle of Christianity! A fair number also live as refugees in Jordan, Lebanon and Syria.

THE GREEK ORTHODOX

One of the largest native Christian communities in the Holy Land is the Greek Orthodox. The higher clergy have tended to be natives of Greece, and Orthodox bishops from Greece or Cyprus are much in evidence on the streets in the Christian Quarter. This church has maintained custodial interests in the great basilicas of the Nativity (Bethlehem) and the Holy Sepulchre and guards these historic rights with great care.

The Greek Orthodox Patriarchate is located within the Christian Quarter on a street of the same name. In his *Guide to the Holy Land*, Father Hoade estimates that ninety local churches and a dozen educational institutions are under its jurisdiction. Those figures have no doubt changed in recent years. A long-simmering internal dispute concerns the Arab Orthodox movement's efforts to have a greater voice in the church. This is the old "local control" issue.

The Greek Orthodox community in the Holy Land is, of course, part of the Orthodox branch of the Christian world, centered in Russia, Eastern Europe, the Balkan countries and the Middle East. It includes some one hundred and fifty million members worldwide.

Of special interest to Westerners is the unique decoration of the interior of Orthodox churches. Often the entire interior, walls and ceilings, are covered with panels of beautiful icons, stylized paintings of Christ and the saints. The altar is behind a wall of such icons, known as an iconostasis. There is a tangible sense that the entire communion of saints, along with the angelic host, is present in the church, especially during the Eucharist.

THE LATINS

After the final defeat of the Crusader kingdom and the mass withdrawal of Western Europeans, the Roman Catholic or, as it is commonly called in the Holy Land, the "Latin" (as distinct from the "Greek") Church became more or less defunct. It had few Arab members at that time. The Franciscan Order stayed on and managed, during centuries of official harassment, to maintain a Western Christian presence at the great shrines. In 1847 the Pope reestablished the Latin Patriarchate of Jerusalem, which had led the church during the era of the Latin Kingdom of Jerusalem.

Franciscan monks, in their customary brown robes, are still present at most of the holy places where they kept vigil through the centuries of Turkish rule.

Today the Latin Patriarchate is one of the largest Christian communities in the region. The worldwide Catholic Church has aided the local community with funds and other resources for many years. An international Catholic organization providing funds from abroad for schools and other projects is the Knights of the Holy Sepulchre. The Catholic Near East Welfare Association, with headquarters in New York, is a major church-sponsored agency for promoting aid to the "Oriental" churches in the Near East. It offers help to Orthodox, Syriac, Coptic and Ethiopian churches, as well as to Catholic organizations.

A number of religious orders of women and of men are active in the Holy Land, some based in the West and some native. Since the first Arab was appointed as a bishop in 1948, the church has attempted to pass leadership more and more to Arabs. This has culminated in the appointment of the current Latin Patriarch, Michel Sabbah, a native of Nazareth. His appointment by the Pope was a brilliant stroke, giving the Palestinians of the Latin rite considerable new recognition and leadership.

Father Hoade estimates that one hundred and seventy Latin church-

The traditional place where the angel announced the glad tidings of Christ's birth to the shepherds, near Bethlehem.

es and chapels exist in the Holy Land, one-third being considered as holy places. He counts one hundred and eighty-six "religious establishments," eight hospitals, eight clinics, and several homes for the aged. Bethlehem University is among these institutions. Again, his numbers may be outdated.

THE GREEK CATHOLICS

Few Western Christians are aware of the Melkite, or Greek Catholic, Church, which has a very large presence among the native Christians in the Holy Land. This church follows the Byzantine liturgy and traditions of the Greek Orthodox Church but is in communion with the Roman Catholic Church. It has substantial membership in other Middle

Eastern countries and in the United States. Its patriarch resides in Syria.

The patriarchal vicar, an archbishop, maintains headquarters on Greek Catholic Patriarchate Road, one of the lanes leading from the Jaffa Gate into the Christian Quarter. The patriarchal church is well worth a visit for its unusual library and bookstore and to experience the beauty of its Byzantine liturgy and icons. Holy Land parishes of this church are located principally in Galilee, which has its own diocese. The Greek Catholic Church (or Melkite Rite) separated from the Orthodox a few centuries ago and established communion with Rome. It is larger in Holy Land membership than the Latin Rite of the Catholic Church.

THE MARONITES

The Maronite Church, largest Christian denomination in Lebanon, has had an historic membership base in Galilee, which is just south of Lebanon. There is a patriarchal vicar in Jerusalem and parishes in Haifa, Nazareth, Acre, El-Jish and Jaffa. This church owes its name to Saint Maron, a saintly hermit who lived in the mountains of Syria about 400 A.D. A major monastic center arose near the place of his burial and became the spiritual center of the region. In the 700s the Maronites chose their first patriarch. Persecution in Syria led the main body of the church to resettle in Lebanon during the ninth century. The church has been in communion with the popes since the era of the Crusades. Although elements of the Latin rite have been introduced, Maronite liturgy and spirituality retain their distinctiveness.

THE ARMENIAN ORTHODOX

This church, more or less unknown to the Western world, has a mighty history. Armenia, nestled in the mountains between Turkey and the Caspian See, lays claim to being the first nation to adopt the religion of Christ *en masse*. About 300 A.D. Saint Gregory the Illuminator, the "father" of this national church, converted the king. Christianity was soon adopted throughout the region. Armenian art and literature developed along with the church, and permeate it today.

In 551, a century after the great ecumenical Council of Chalcedon, the Armenian Church formally rejected the council's doctrine concerning the twofold nature of Christ, divine and human. Churches which rejected the council are known as non-Chalcedonian Orthodox, or monophysites (one nature-ites). They are not in communion with either Constantinople (Greek Orthodoxy) or Rome. They are sometimes referred to as Oriental Orthodox, to distinguish them from the Eastern Orthodox.

From the earliest times, the Armenians were drawn to the Holy Land and established many churches and institutions there. They were closely allied with the Greek Orthodox and the Byzantine Empire as long as the latter lasted. As early as the 600s they had no fewer than seventy convents in the Holy Land. Partly through good relations with the Turkish sultans, the Armenian Church managed to establish itself as co-custodian of the great basilicas, along with the Greeks and the Latins. That special status exists even today, which is quite amazing considering the small role Armenia plays in the Christian world.

The separate Armenian altar in the Church of the Nativity in Bethlehem, just to the left of the main Greek altar, gives an impression of austerity which is in remarkable contrast to the richly decorated Greek Orthodox altar. The black-robed Armenian priests wear a hooded headpiece, which distinguishes them from all others in the Holy Land.

As noted earlier, the Armenian is the only church to have its own quarter in the Old City. In addition to a few commercial establishments it contains a museum, library, schools, monastery and, in the opinion of many, Jerusalem's most beautiful church, Saint James, the cathedral of the Armenian Patriarch of Jerusalem, named after the apostle who became the first leader (bishop) of Jerusalem.

Armenia suffered over a million deaths in the Turkish genocide at the time of the First World War, only to be absorbed later by the Soviet Union. Now that it is once again an independent country and free to practice its religion, it would not be surprising if Armenian pilgrimages to Jerusalem were on the rise. Millions of Armenians living in the diaspora, newly prosperous, may also be expected to contribute to a strengthening of the Armenian Church's ancient presence in the Holy Land.

The Syrian Orthodox

This ancient church has also maintained a membership base in the Holy Land since early times. Often called "Jacobites," the Syrian Church can trace itself back to first century Antioch, where people first used the name "Christian" for disciples of Jesus. (Acts 11:26) This area was also the cradle of the sacred liturgy, which later spread to Constantinople and elsewhere. The Syrian Church contributed vastly to theology and early missionary work. A split arose in the church over the human versus divine nature of Christ in the fifth century. The Syrian Church took the monophysite side, thereby separating itself from both Rome and Constantinople. A minority of the Syrian Church has since come into communion with Rome, while the Syrian Orthodox are said to be in dialogue with both Rome and the Greek Orthodox.

The Coptic Orthodox

This is the church of Egypt, tracing its history to the early missionary work of St. Mark. The liturgy is in Coptic, the ancient language of

Egypt, but scripture readings and prayers are in Arabic. The Copts have historically been monophysite (one nature in Christ) but have come very close to communion with Rome on a number of occasions. The differences today are mostly semantic. Their spiritual leader, Pope Shenouda III, met with Catholic Pope Paul VI in 1973, at which time they issued a common declaration of faith. The church has had no end of difficulties, existing as it has for thirteen hundred years under the thumb of the Muslim majority in Egypt. Yet, even today, there are an estimated 7,000,000 to 9,000,000 Coptic Christians in Egypt, demonstrating an amazing staying power.

During the period of Mameluke (Egyptian) rule following the Crusades, the Copts were favored over other indigenous Christian groups and began to accumulate custodial rights in some of the holy places in Jerusalem. They have a clerical residence in the Holy Sepulchre and certain specific rights to formal worship in this and other major shrines. Notably, as pointed out earlier, they preside over a small chapel covering one end of Christ's tomb. Given the proximity of Jerusalem to Egypt, where millions of Copts live, it is possible that they will be more in evidence in the future, if peace and prosperity in the region open up the arteries of travel.

THE ETHIOPIAN ORTHODOX

The unique Ethiopian Church has maintained institutions in Jerusalem from Byzantine times. Throughout the centuries, this isolated Christian nation in North Africa, surrounded by Islam, has sent pilgrims to Jerusalem. Even today some come from the Ethiopian capital of Addis Ababa for the colorful service on Holy Saturday night on the roof of Deir-es-Sultan, the Empress Helena's Church, attached to the Holy Sepulchre. During a ritual called Searching for the Body of Christ the

priests wander about in the dark carrying candles to the rhythm of cere-
monial drums. One may enter the Ethiopian compound through a door
and stairway off the courtyard in front of the Holy Sepulchre. A water
well identified with the Empress Helena may be viewed, and one may
walk upstairs to the humble rooftop quarters and chapel of the gentle
Ethiopian monks. A small contribution would be welcome help in their
struggle to survive.

Cut off by the Islamic world from all Christians except the Copts of
Egypt, their sponsors in the faith, the Ethiopian Church developed some
unusual ways. Freshly baked, warm bread is used in the eucharist, which
requires five celebrants, two of them priests. Certain Jewish customs are
practiced, including the Sabbath, circumcision, the offering of fresh
fruits, and rules regarding food. In their churches there is kept a sacred
object representing the Ark of the Covenant.

The Ethiopian Church is non-Chalcedonian (monophysite)
Orthodox, like the Armenians, Copts and Syrian Jacobites. There is a
huge priesthood, possibly numbering 200,000, and a total church membership in Ethiopia of some 17,000,000. Although the church's presence
in Jerusalem today is small and impoverished, who can say whether
changing conditions might result in an infusion of new blood, given that
this is the single largest national church in the region.

THE PROTESTANT CHURCHES

Among Protestant churches represented today in the Holy Land are
the following: Anglican, Scottish, Lutheran, Quakers, Southern Baptist,
Bible Baptist, Nazarenes, Pentecostal, Seventh Day Adventists, Church of
Christ, Brethren, Mennonites and the International Evangelical Church,
according to Hoade's *Guide to the Holy Land*. (The list is somewhat out
of date.) A number of nondenominational institutions are also active.

The Anglican Church, which has had a bishop in Jerusalem for a long time, is the largest in local membership, followed by the Lutherans, whose Holy Land institutions are mainly German. Evangelicals from the United States are attracted to Jerusalem in great numbers, as discussed in Chapter 3. The Anglicans operate churches in Jerusalem and else-where, including Saint George Cathedral, and are well established in the country. Both Anglicans and Lutherans have Arab congregations and promote the social welfare of the Arab people without regard to religious affiliation.

The Southern Baptist Convention is one of the most active Protestant bodies, with a number of churches around the country as well as other establishments. Two other Protestant institutions of note are the American Colony, a utopian community established a century ago, which still performs charitable activities in Jerusalem, centered near the Damascus Gate, and the YMCA. The main "Y," across the street from the King David Hotel, is the tallest and one of the largest buildings in Jerusalem. A more typical "Y" is located near the Anglican complex of Saint George outside Damascus Gate. Both are busy religious and social centers. The Swedish Christian Study Centre, just inside Jaffa Gate, is a good place for pilgrims to stop for information on Jerusalem and its churches. The Centre also promotes interfaith dialogue and Arab-Israeli reconciliation.

Justice cannot be done here to the many other church groups, European and American, which are active in missionary or charitable enterprises in the Holy Land today. The Mormons, the International Christian Embassy and the Quakers deserve special mention. Some of these denominations have no native membership base to speak of, but engage in proselytizing, and educational and charitable works.

THE EMIGRATION CRISIS

Much has been written about the gradual shrinkage of the once-vibrant Christian Palestinian population within the Holy Land. We will content ourselves with the observations of two students of this trend. May their sense of urgency be translated into effective countermeasures. Perhaps someone reading this may have part of the answer.

In his sympathetic portrait of these descendants of the church described in the Acts of the Apostles, Kenneth Cragg, in *The Arab Christian, A History in the Middle East*, says:

> A variety of factors are leading to the steady attrition of the Arab Christian communities in the region. There is therefore an urgency about perception of them in the West lest the aura of "the Holy Land" should lead us to think of a spiritual museum rather than of living, dying people in the throes of a deep struggle for survival and fulfillment.
>
> Whatever the reasons for the continuing emigration over the last generation—and there are no doubt a combination of economic, political, and cultural factors—the result could be devastating to the relationship of Christianity to the sacred places of the Gospel. Some blame the continuing exodus on rising Islamic fundamentalism, others on the anti-terrorist policies of Israel itself.

While Christian pilgrims can do very little directly to counter the influence of the radical terrorist movement known as Hamas, or to modify Israeli policies concerning land, travel, housing, schools, and jobs, there may be less dramatic actions which could, collectively, give hope to the native Arab Christian people. For, to quote Wilken again:

> Without the presence of living Christian communities, the witness of the Holy Land can only be equivocal. The martyrs and teachers, the monks and bishops, the faithful who lived in Bethlehem and Beit Jala and Nazareth and Jerusalem would no longer be signs of a living faith, but forgotten names from a distant past. Bethlehem would become a

shrine, and Christian Jerusalem a city of ancient renown. Only people, not stones and earth and marble, can bear an authentic witness.

As a beginning, we who travel to their Holy Land can offer them our prayers, our moral support and our financial support. A few tour groups already are arranging opportunities to meet and get acquainted with our Palestinian Christian sisters and brothers. Ways to pursue this idea are described in Chapter 15.

An outstanding videotape documenting the plight of the 150,000 or so remaining Palestinian Christians, entitled "Turning Point: Crisis in the Holy Land," is available from the Holy Land Foundation, 1400 Quincy, N.E., Washington, D.C. 20017.

10.

The Jews In The Holy Land Today
Heinz 57 Varieties

lthough a small country, Israel includes three major cities: Tel Aviv, Haifa and Jerusalem. Tel Aviv has been called, with typical Jewish humor, the Big Orange. It is, indeed, New York City on the Mediterranean, or perhaps Miami Beach East. There is an impressive skyline along a beach which extends for miles, and hotels standing shoulder to shoulder. It is a big, bustling, modern city, almost entirely inhabited by Jews. The mostly Arab city of Jaffa (Joppa) abuts it on the south. The two constitute one metropolitan area.

Haifa probably has the distinction of being the most beautiful of Israeli cities. Situated on Mount Carmel, overlooking the Mediterranean near the northern end of the country, its modern skyscrapers cling to the sides of its numerous hills, many having enviable views of the sea. There is something dreamy about the city, like San Francisco. It is primarily inhabited by Jews. As in Tel Aviv, the population is principally secular, or nonobservant Jews. Arab Christians, Muslims and Druze also reside in Haifa in significant numbers and live peacefully together with the Jews.

Jerusalem, as discussed more fully elsewhere, is really two cities side by side, one Jewish, one Arab, divided by an imaginary line. West Jerusalem, the larger part of the city, is Jewish.

This modern city sprawls up and down the Judean hills. It has old neighborhoods and fabulous new apartment complexes and shopping centers. To live in this city is the dream of vast numbers of Jews around the world. This is not because of its climate or its tranquility, but rather because of its defining importance in Jewish identity.

THE COMING OF MODERN ISRAEL

While a Jewish community always lived in Jerusalem and in Galilee during the Ottoman era, immigration began in earnest during the latter part of the nineteenth century. Land was purchased and immigration financed by Jewish groups in Europe. As this Zionist movement, intent upon reestablishing a Jewish homeland, gained strength, the numbers of immigrants and their purchases of land began to cause alarm among the Arab population of what was then called Palestine, a neglected outpost of the Ottoman (Turkish) Empire.

The call for a Jewish "homeland" in Palestine received a big boost from an endorsement by Britain's Lord Balfour, in what is known as the Balfour Declaration, at the time of the First World War. Eventually the increasing number of Jews and their major land acquisitions provoked hostility on the part of the local Arabs, who could see what was happening. The British Mandate Government sought to suppress the Jewish efforts, leading to the creation of the Haganah, a Jewish civilian defense force. Two Jewish factions waged guerrilla warfare against the

Mandate Government and the Arabs. Some of modern Israel's greatest leaders were once considered "terrorists" by Britain, most notably Menachem Begin.

The Nazi genocide against European Jewry, known as the Holocaust, with its 6,000,000 victims, provided the final impetus for the creation of the State of Israel in 1948. Anyone who has seen the movie *Exodus* has an understanding of the tumultuous days of the birth of the nation and the new hope it gave to the demoralized Jews of the post-war world.

THE JEWISH POPULATION

The Jewish population today is an ingathering of people from over eighty countries. Most had to learn the "dead" language, Hebrew, the official language of Israel. Although all speak Hebrew now, their national backgrounds remain important to an understanding of the country, as do their religious practices. Since most non-Jews are unaware of the history of the Jews over the centuries of the diaspora, it is worth pointing out that there are three main groups, in terms of cultural origin. They are the Ashkenazim, the Sephardim and the Orientals. The first group trace their background to Jewish communities in Germany, Poland, Russia and other nations of central and eastern Europe, who once spoke Yiddish, a blend of German and Hebrew. Many Hassidim, a pious movement within the Ashkenazim, immigrated to Palestine in the 1700s.

The Sephardim are descendants of Jews who were expelled *en masse* from Spain in 1492 and emigrated to Southeastern Europe. Many settled in Constantinople. Their traditional language was Ladino, a mixture of Spanish and Hebrew.

The so-called Orientals have emigrated from Middle Eastern

A modern Jewish settlement on the West Bank.

countries, such as Yemen, Iraq, Iran and Afghanistan. Each of these groups naturally brought along much of the culture of the countries where they had lived for centuries.

CIVIL RELIGION

Although the majority of Israeli Jews are "nonobservant," virtually all adhere to the civil religion of the country, by which is meant a deep reverence for everything connected with the history of the Jewish people. The very land is holy, even to nonbelievers. The nation itself is considered sacred. Places like Masada, the great natural fortress defended to the death against the Roman army in 73 A.D., are beloved in a quasi-religious way.

There is a peculiar coming together of God and nation worship in

Judaism because through the covenant with Abraham the Lord made the Jews his special people and gave them this land in perpetuity.

Yad Vashem, the monumental memorial to the six million victims of the Holocaust, stands amid military and civilian cemeteries on Mount Herzl, to the west of Jerusalem. It is equally prominent on the list of sacred places for Israeli Jews, and for good reason.

The most sacred spot is, of course, the Western Wall of the Temple Mount, described elsewhere. Although it is the remnant of the retaining wall of the Second Temple, a uniquely religious place, its reverent Jewish visitors include those who put no stock in divine revelation. And why not? It evokes memories of the glorious, as well as the tragic, periods of Jewish national history.

VARIETIES OF RELIGIOUS PRACTICE

In West Jerusalem there are "Heinz 57" varieties of Jews. Amos Elon speaks of "walls within walls, enclaves within enclaves, ghettos within ghettos." Some neighborhoods are mostly secular, while others, such as Mea Shearim, are ultra-Orthodox Jewish fundamentalists. There are even "ultra-ultra" Orthodox groups who deny the legitimacy of the Israeli State itself, considering it a sort of sacrilege.

Some groups will not serve in the country's military. Some oppose the use of Hebrew except for prayer, and insist upon speaking Yiddish. While the Sabbath, from sundown on Friday until sundown on Saturday, is honored by all Israeli Jews, including the secular, it is enforced rigidly in Orthodox neighborhoods. Virtually nothing moves, except for religious purposes. Violators have been taunted, even stoned, in the more extreme neighborhoods.

There are over a thousand synagogues in Jerusalem. On Friday evening they are filled. Restaurants are closed, as are movie houses.

Buses do not roll. Blue laws prevail. Elon gives a feel for the rich ethnic variety when Jews pray in Jerusalem:

> Certain synagogues serve Polish congregants; others follow only the German, Lithuanian, Hungarian, or so-called Anglo-Saxon rites of their members. Among the Sephardic, certain synagogues are dedicated to...the different rites of Italy, Kurdistan, and Morocco, as well as of Istanbul, Cairo, San'a (Yemen), Tangier, Salonika, Sarajevo, and Sofia. Some Ashkenazic rabbis still dress like Polish noblemen of the eighteenth century, in black coats, black or white leggings and—on holidays—majestic fur hats....

Apart from the dissenting ultra-Orthodox, there are the merely Orthodox, led by the chief rabbinate. This body has jurisdiction over marriage and questions as to who is entitled to be considered a Jew. Reform Judaism is frowned upon. The chief rabbinate is also responsible for overseeing ritual baths, kosher slaughterhouses and rabbinical courts. Their authority is always disputed by the ultra-Orthodox, and the historic animosities among fervently religious Jewish sects are every bit as impassioned and regrettable as have been the conflicts among pious Christian groups. Such is human nature, even among the devout.

Some of the above may leave a negative impression of Jewish religious life in Israel. That feeling must be balanced by a realization that it is easier to describe the externals of any religion than the interior spirituality of the individual people practicing the religion. In this case the reality is that Jerusalem is full of Jews who devote their lives to studying the scriptures and worshipping the God of Abraham, Isaac and Jacob, that is to say the same God we Christians love and worship. Their customs are historically conditioned, very human, and occasionally hard for an outsider to appreciate. Exactly the same may be said of our own rich heritage of customs. We owe them our understanding, our respect and, especially, our friendship and commitment to their survival.

11.

The Muslims In The Holy Land Today
People, Not Stereotypes

Most of the Muslims of Israel, the West Bank (called Judea and Samaria by Israel) and the Gaza Strip, or, as they would prefer to call the entire area, Palestine, are descendants of people who inhabited the land prior to the Muslim conquest in the 600s. During the five centuries between the Muslim conquest and the Crusades, the majority of city and village dwellers gradually converted from the church to the mosque. Of course, many of the nomads had not been Christianized to begin with. These, known as Bedouins, live in large tents and move around with their flocks, even today. The majority of the Arabs are either villagers or city dwellers. Western dress is common, but Palestinian peasant dress can be seen and a return to Muslim dress has accompanied the rise of fundamentalism.

Most of the two million Muslims in the country are of the Sunni

Street scene, "Old City" of Jerusalem.

branch of Islam, of which there are four rites. The majority here belong to the Shafi'i rite. Muslim courts deal with matters of personal status, such as marriage, divorce and inheritance. A large number of Druse, a religion related to Islam, live in the northern part of Israel, known as Galilee. They are considered great soldiers and have been loyal allies of Israel's Jews. A minority of the Muslims belong to the Shiite branch of Islam or to small, independent sects.

ISLAM

For those unfamiliar with the religion, it may be necessary to provide some explanation of the faith. Islam is a radically monotheistic religion practiced by about a billion people in the Middle East, northern Africa, and southern Asia. It is the largest religion in the world after

Christianity. It came into being in the early 600s when Mohammed, a merchant in Arabia, began to receive what he claimed to be divine revelations through the mediation of the angel Gabriel. These messages were written down over a period of years and compiled into the Muslim scriptures, known as the Koran, or Quran.

The name of the religion, Islam, means "to submit," or surrender oneself to the will and grace of God, called, in Arabic, Allah. The Koran acknowledges revelations to Abraham, Moses, Jesus and many other "prophets." It considers the Bible divinely revealed but considers the Koran the last word of prophecy, and Mohammed the Seal of the Prophets.

Where there is contradiction between the Bible and the Koran, Islamic scholars conclude that the older scriptures have been corrupted by men. Mohammed lived close enough to Byzantine Palestine to have been conversant with Christianity and Judaism, and there are major elements of both in the Koran. A misunderstanding of the Christian doctrine of the Trinity seems apparent to us in the Koran, which assumes Christians worship the Father, Jesus Christ and Mary as three gods. Even the notion of three "persons" within one God (Father, Son and Holy Spirit), however, would be unacceptable to Islam, in light of its insistence on the absolutely unitary nature of the godhead.

They do share with Christians the understanding of God as omnipotent, omniscient, all merciful and all holy, and as the creator and judge of all. Jesus is revered as a very great prophet, but his crucifixion, resurrection and divinity are rejected by the Koran. His mother, the Virgin Mary, has a special place in Muslim piety, possibly reflecting the universal and intense devotion to her in the Christian world of Mohammed's time.

The five "pillars" of Islam are the profession of faith in Allah and his prophet Mohammed, prayer five times a day, alms-giving, fasting from daylight to sundown during the month of Ramadan, and, if possible, a pilgrimage or hajj to Mecca during one's lifetime. Friday is the Muslim equivalent of the Sabbath. Prayer services are held in the mosques, which are not open to non-Muslims during such times.

The Song of the Muezzin

Of all the manifestations of Islam a tourist will encounter, the most chilling and yet serenely beautiful is the call to prayer. The faithful are summoned five times a day by a muezzin or prayer leader, chanting from the top of a tower called a minaret. This practice goes on everywhere in the Muslim world, always in Arabic, but Westerners are most likely to encounter it while in Jerusalem.

The song of the muezzin is a lilting, passionate call to prayer, a haunting sound which may awaken you before dawn and signal the end of your day. The custom reminds one of the Angelus prayer, which for centuries was signaled in villages across Europe by the tolling of church bells at 6:00 a.m., 12:00 noon and 6:00 p.m. Formal Muslim prayer is at dawn, midday, midafternoon, sunset and evening.

Today the muezzin no longer has to climb up to the balcony of the minaret to issue the call to prayer. Four speakers, aiming in all directions, are mounted on the minaret. His voice can be heard a long way as he chants into a microphone with the volume set quite high. You may even be listening to a tape! In Jerusalem one is likely to be able to hear two or three muezzins at once, chanting from different neighborhoods. If you are in your room you will probably open the window, look out into the city, and wonder at this mystical sound. After a recitation from the Koran the muezzin will intone the seven phrases of the invitation to prayer, singing in Arabic, of course:

God is great! God is great!

I attest that there is no god except God.

I attest that Mohammed is the chosen of God.

Arise! (Come) to pray,

Arise! (Come) to salvation.

God is great! God is great!

There is not god but God.

The tones, melodies and length of the chant may vary. In his little book, *The Song of the Muezzin*, Sabino De Sandoli recalls hearing the daybreak call begun by one muezzin "using a grave, soft voice, and in a mode so delicate as if he wished to accompany the sleep of the faithful rather than to disturb them," followed after a few minutes of silence by a "stupendous baritone voice," and, after a pause, by a third muezzin singing in a sustained tenor voice. If we need reminders to turn our hearts to the Lord in prayer, we get them five times a day in the Holy Land.

The stereotype of the radical, frenzied fundamentalist does not at all fit most of the millions of people who daily pray to Allah. Many kindly and innocent Muslims are sensitive to the negative image their religion has in the Western world. The unresolved question is whether they will be able to prevail over the well-organized fanatic minority.

12.

Relations Among Christian Communities
Beginning of Mutual Respect

After centuries during which the minority Christian communities of Jerusalem and the rest of the Holy Land have lived in relative isolation from one another, the spirit of unity has begun to take hold. As recently as a generation ago there was little contact between, and less cooperation among the Greeks, Latins, Anglicans, Lutherans, Armenians, Copts, Syrians and Ethiopians. Rights in the shrines were jealously guarded against one another. That is slowly changing but needs a few more good shoves from the Holy Spirit. One would think that shunned and persecuted Christian minorities under Turkish rule would have come together for mutual support, but they were too busy fighting over crumbs.

Greek and Latin monks have literally come to blows in the past over the symbolic right to sweep floors and dust lamps in disputed areas of

Close-up of the Star in the Cave of the Nativity in Bethlehem.

the Church of the Nativity and the Basilica of the Holy Sepulchre. Armenians, Georgians and Greeks often used their influence with the Ottoman Turkish government in Istanbul (formerly Constantinople) to gain more control over shrines. The major powers of Europe, especially France (Catholic), Austria (Catholic), and Russia (Orthodox) used every diplomatic tool at their disposal to obtain rights for their coreligionists vis-a-vis the rival churches. All of this culminated in the "Status Quo," a nineteenth century edict or "firman" of the Ottoman Court in Istanbul, settling the competing rights of rival churches in the holy places. The "Status Quo" is still in effect, long after the demise of the Ottoman Empire.

Even today certain areas within the great shrines "belong" to the Greeks, or Armenians, or Latins. Possibly the only positive thing that can be said of this scandal is that the tenacity of the rival churches may have prevented the shrines from all becoming mosques during the past several centuries.

Exactly that happened to one of the greatest of the early shrines, the Church of the Ascension, on the very top of the Mount of Olives, built over the place associated by the early Christians with Jesus' ascension to the Father in heaven. Upon the fall of Jerusalem to Saladin in 1187, the ancient church was at once transformed into a mosque. Every year the Franciscans celebrate Ascension Thursday at the remains of the church, with the permission of the Muslim guardians. The Greeks, Armenians, Copts and Syrians celebrate nearby, all on temporary altars. There are hooks on the wall, indicating the space allocated to each community.

No mention has been made of Anglican, Lutheran, Baptist or other Protestant worship at this site, of course, since that would be a novel idea in the land of the Status Quo. The editor of *Catholic Near East* magazine, in response to a letter advocating a greater sharing of all the great churches standing over the holy places associated with Jesus Christ, replied as follows: "You are not the first to note the 'proprietary attitude' of the custodians of the holy places, and, alas, I fear you will not be the last. And yes, our Protestant brethren are overlooked. I am afraid, however, that such a meeting will be a long time in coming. Unfortunately the Holy Land is not the place to find Christian unity and love. We must pray for those, as we do for peace in that troubled region."

Christians are people of hope, so we will hope and pray for change, and a new consciousness does seem to be arising. In 1994 the First International Conference on the Christian Heritage of the Holy Land was held in Jerusalem. The program for this week-long conference reveals that much groundwork has already been done. After an opening reception at the inter-denominational Swedish Christian Study Centre inside Jaffa Gate, the program began at the Catholic-sponsored Notre Dame Center and proceeded to the Tantur Ecumenical Institute outside of Bethlehem. The first speaker was a Dominican scholar and archeologist from the Ecole Biblique of Jerusalem. Subsequent speakers included British church historians of the Holy Land, a religious studies professor from Lund University in Sweden, more British (presumably Anglican or Protestant) scholars, representatives of the Armenian Patriarchate, a Franciscan specialist on Holy Land archeology, a Greek Melkite priest, scholars on Greek Orthodoxy and the Russian, Coptic and Ethiopian churches in the Holy Land, an American Episcopalian expert on the nineteenth century English Protestant community in the Holy Land, a speaker from the (Arab Catholic) Bethlehem University, the dean of Saint George's Anglican Cathedral in Jerusalem and a speaker on the Lutheran community in the Holy Land. The proceedings have been published in book form as *The Christian Heritage in the Holy Land*.

In addition to conflicts among the historic Holy Land churches, there has been tension between the foreign leadership of many churches and their largely Palestinian congregations. This has been notable within Greek Orthodoxy, wherein an Arab movement arose some years ago. As a result, the native Christians have obtained more say in the church. Similar sentiments may have contributed to the elevation of the first Arab to the position of Latin Patriarch of Jerusalem. His Beatitude Michel Sabbah has become a strong voice for Arab Christians.

According to Glenn Bowman, in his monograph entitled "Nationalising the Sacred," foreign-led churches have tended to protect their institutional rights rather than their Palestinian flocks when interests diverged. The Greek (Melkite) Catholic Church and the Anglican Church, "having few Holy Land monuments to maintain for foreign visitors," have strongly supported their Palestinian congregations. They are led by Arab bishops. An example of the opposite, pointed out by Bowman, was the conversion by one church of the only hospital in the Old City to a hotel for its pilgrim visitors.

The Arab Christians, according to Bowman, have recently become more conscious of their national identity as Palestinians and are beginning to think of themselves as Palestinian Christians rather than exclusively as Orthodox or Latin or Anglican, for example. This lowering of the denominational walls should lead to greater inter-church cooperation.

Probably the most hopeful development auguring for future friendship and cooperation among the Christians of the Holy Land is the beginning of regular monthly meetings of the heads of the Christian churches. In 1994 twelve influential church leaders met to discuss the status of Jerusalem and the situation of the churches. They issued a comprehensive and unprecedented statement of their common views and hopes for the future. The signers were the following:

Greek Orthodox Patriarch of Jerusalem

Latin Patriarch of Jerusalem

Armenian Patriarch of Jerusalem

Custos of the Holy Land

Coptic Archbishop of Jerusalem

Syriac Archbishop of Jerusalem

Ethiopian Archbishop of Jerusalem

Anglican Bishop in Jerusalem

Greek Catholic Patriarchal Vicar

Lutheran Bishop of Jerusalem

Maronite Patriarchal Vicar of Jerusalem

Catholic Syriac Patriarchal Vicar of Jerusalem

The following is an excerpt from their joint statement:

> The Christians of the entire world, Western or Eastern, should have the right to come on pilgrimage to Jerusalem. They ought to be able to find there all that is necessary to carry out their pilgrimage in the spirit of their authentic tradition: freedom to visit and to move around, to pray at holy sites, to embark on the spiritual attendance and respectful practice of their faith, to enjoy the possibility of a prolonged stay and the benefits of hospitality and dignified lodgings.

Also in 1994, the three church leaders who are responsible for the care of the Holy Sepulchre (the Greek Orthodox Patriarch, the Franciscan Custos of the Holy Land, and the Armenian Patriarch) finally approved a common design for the redecoration of the great dome of the rotunda over the tomb of Christ. This represented the first time they had been able to reach a consensus on such a joint activity since the imposition of the Status Quo by the Turks!

Jesus said the world will know you are my disciples by your love for one another (John 13:34-35). Certainly their Muslim neighbors have not had much cause to be edified by the love between Holy Land Christian communities in the recent past. But the Spirit is "a-moving." Maybe Isabelle Bacon, writing as a Reformed Christian in *Walking Beside Jesus in the Holy Land*, spoke prophetically when she expressed the fond hope that one day there would be a Protestant chapel in the Church of the Holy Sepulchre.

Indeed, it is time for the multitude of Protestant pilgrims of every denomination to share in the joy of public worship in this most sacred of places. It has been the preeminent place to revere the crucifixion and resurrection since the early days of the Church. In a sense it belongs to all who worship Christ as the Risen Savior and Son of God.

It has been argued that permitting numerous additional church bodies to conduct services at the Holy Sepulchre would be impractical because there are so many. Good order would require careful planning and scheduling, but it should not be impossible to improve upon the present situation. The Anglican Communion and the Lutheran Church already participate in meetings with the custodial churches.

It has also been suggested that further sharing must await full unity of faith. If that were essential to sharing the holy places, then Orthodox, Catholic and Armenian churches could not share the sites as they already do. It is submitted that acts of good will, such as sharing the great shrines, are a Christian mandate and may well be a step towards greater unity.

13.

Rival Claims To The Holy Land
A Divine Dilemma

A s has been demonstrated in the course of this book, Jerusalem and its hinterland, as well as Galilee in the north, and the entire stretch of desert and mountains and coastal plains we Christians call the Holy Land, is also a sacred place to Jews and Muslims. In addition, it is the ancient homeland of two peoples. Its political and military history has often been a struggle for control and survival among these religions and peoples.

Many Christian pilgrims stay at hospices around the Jaffa Gate, near the Holy Sepulchre and the headquarters of the Greek Orthodox Patriarch, the Latin Patriarch, the Greek Catholic Patriarchal Vicar and the Armenian Patriarch. As they come through the gate they must pass right by the Tower of David and the Citadel built by King Herod. This is David's city! He made it the Hebrew capital three thousand years ago.

153

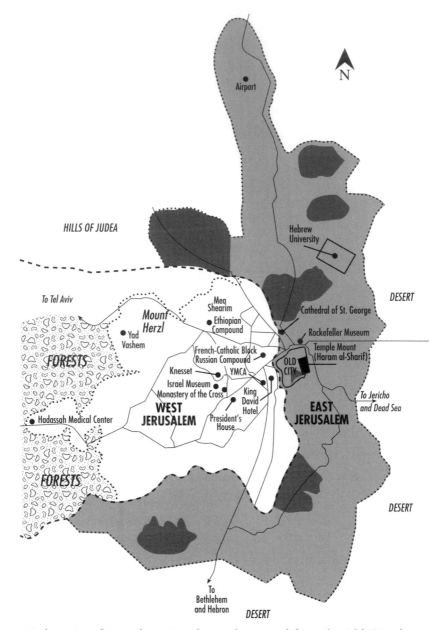

Modern city of Jerusalem. Note how it has spread from the Old City during the last century. White is Jewish West Jerusalem; gray is Arab East Jerusalem; black represents recent Jewish developments within East Jerusalem.

Some of the Palestinians' ancestors were here even before David. One of their champions was a giant of a man named Goliath, the one slain by David. To be precise, Goliath was a Philistine. This early people inhabited a string of cities along the Mediterranean coast south of modern Tel Aviv-Jaffa, including the Gaza Strip, which now is home to nearly a million Palestinians. The name Palestine is believed to derive from the word Philistine. For Palestinians, Christians as well as Muslims, Jerusalem is not simply a special place; it is El Quds, The Holy. It is the Dwelling of The Holy One, El-Qudoous. This is verified by Palestinian Christian leader Elias Chacour.

How can these conflicting claims be resolved? Perhaps first we need to concede that the Israeli government has accorded more respect to Christian pilgrims than has any government since the Crusades. The precarious status of Christian institutions under the Turks is no more. Churches are relatively free to build and repair shrines and are given free rein compared to the past. Under Jordanian rule, from 1948 to 1967, the Old City was off limits to Jews, and sometimes to Christians. The Jewish quarter was largely destroyed, their cemeteries vandalized and their right to visit the Western Wall denied. There was in effect, of course, a state of war between Israel and Jordan.

Today the Muslims occupy the Temple Mount, including the Dome of the Rock and Al-Aksa Mosque, which sit on the very site of the two great Jewish temples. West Bank residents are frequently blocked from entering Israel, however. Israel maintains it can be trusted to administer the Old City for residents and pilgrims of all three monotheistic faiths. Critics say that is wishful thinking.

It would certainly require a great increase in the level of trust between Israel and Palestinians. As of today that seems unlikely. Still, it is good to be able to report that there are peace-oriented bilateral groups here and there in Israel and the West Bank, dialoguing and acting in concert to create an atmosphere of trust. They face an uphill battle.

The Jews' special attachment to the land is based on God's covenant gift of the land to Abraham, Isaac, Jacob and their descendants. This claim is expressed in the notion of "Eretz Israel" (literally "The Land of Israel"), a reverence for the very soil promised forever by God himself.

This is not altogether different from the Christian reverence for this land where Jesus, the Redeemer, the God Man, walked, ate, rested, preached, and died. Such an incarnational feeling extends to the pavement stones and the hillsides, the dirt paths and the desert, because Jesus may have walked that way. He is not known to have sped around in a Toyota, or even on horseback. He trod the landscape on foot. Perhaps even barefoot at times. The whole country was rendered sacramental, something made holy forever by association with Jesus, the Suffering Servant, the Lamb of God, the Perfect Sacrifice, the Word Made Flesh.

The Palestinian people have a strong political claim to a homeland, having lived there for millennia, although nearly always powerless and ruled by outsiders. Both Muslim and Christian Palestinians want a homeland, a state of their own, and there are indications this awakened nationalism is building kinship across their sectarian boundaries. Observers have commented upon the increased participation by Muslims in the Latin Palm Sunday procession down the Mount of Olives and the Greek Orthodox ceremony of the Holy Fire.

A new organization, called the Center for Religious and Heritage Studies in the Holy Land, is dedicated to Muslim-Christian dialogue, especially among the Palestinians themselves. The literature of the Center is clearly intended to promote a common feeling of Palestinian patriotism, crossing religious lines. One article, for example, points out "common Arab feasts," noting that Muslims participate in the celebration of Christmas in Bethlehem, that many Palestinian establishments close on both Fridays and Sundays, that Muslims dye eggs for Easter, and that many Christians are invited by Muslim friends to share dinner during the holy month of Ramadan.

The churches are promoting this same feeling of camaraderie by extending their educational programs to include Muslims, with no proselytizing motive at all. An outstanding example is Prophet Elias College in Ibellin, a Galilean village near Haifa. This school, begun in 1981 by a dynamic Greek Catholic Arab priest, Abuna Elias Chacour, serves a mixed student body of Christians, Muslims and Druse. The faculty includes all these, plus some Jewish teachers, and the school seeks to recruit Jewish students as well. Although officially Christian, the college invites everyone, and obviously seeks to set an example of openness for others. Following a 1996 terrorist attack in Tel Aviv, hundreds of Arab students at the college donated blood for their injured Jewish "blood brothers" as an act of solidarity.

On a hill outside Bethlehem is the Tantur Ecumenical Institute for Theological Studies which, through its lectures and courses, promotes Christian unity, inter-church harmony and intercultural dialogue among Jews, Muslims and Christians. For information on its programs, write Tantur at: P.O. Box 19556, Jerusalem 91194 Israel; or fax them at 972-2-760914.

Israeli peace groups play an important, if unofficial, role in promoting reconciliation between Jews and Arabs. One example, cited in *The Arab Christian*, is the Jewish-Palestinian enterprise known in Hebrew as Neve Shalom, in Arabic as Wahat al-Salam, in English as Oasis of Peace. Located on the frontier between Israel and the West Bank, it promotes a vision of future harmony between Jews and Arabs. The community

Sheep grazing outside an abandoned Palestinian refugee camp.

consists of Jews and Arabs, both Christian and Muslim, trying to live together as equals, acting as leaven in their respective communities.

Palestinian leader Yasser Arafat has made overt gestures towards the Christians among the Palestinians. He has made it a point to visit Christian schools and has announced that Christmas and Easter will be national holidays in the territories turned over to Palestinian rule. Whether native Christians will fare well under Palestinian rule remains to be seen.

The consensus of the major Christian bodies in the Holy Land is clear: there needs to be an internationally enforceable guarantee of permanent access to their holy places by people from all nations and all three religions; the religions must have ownership and control of their own churches, mosques and synagogues; visitors must have access to living accommodations and the opportunity to remain in the Holy Land for extended stays; and the rights of local religious groups must be equally respected. This is a tall order, but certainly not an unreasonable goal. It would require a multinational, multireligious permanent authority, perhaps sanctioned by the United Nations. The shape it should take cannot be foreseen at this time.

To quote from a sermon delivered by the Lord to an assemblage of Muslims, Jews and Christians on the Temple Mount in the beautiful, book-length parable *Joshua in the Holy Land*:

> If only you can learn to get along and help each other, and work together, this little country will become the showpiece and the model for all the world; she will be the light unto the nations.

Part Four

NOW, ABOUT YOUR TRIP

14.

Preparing For A Pilgrimage

B y "preparing" we mean spiritual preparation. For detailed information on weather, what clothes to bring, the exchange rate of shekels, restaurants, and how to say "Where is the rest room?" the reader is referred to standard travel guidebooks on Israel, available at bookstores. For detailed pilgrim itineraries, covering all the religious shrines in the country, the reader is referred to specialized guidebooks on the holy places. Some of these are listed at the end of this book.

THE SOCIAL DIMENSION

If possible, meet and get acquainted with others who will be sharing your pilgrimage. If the trip is sponsored by a local congregation, this will be a fairly easy task, and the church may well organize a get-together before departure. If you are traveling with a tour which advertises nationally, you most likely will have no opportunity to meet your fellow pilgrims beforehand. You might, nevertheless, be able to persuade the tour company to circulate a list of the participants so each can become familiar with names and home cities. That would help break the ice. Some tour companies are reluctant to share this information, however.

Where a group from a local church is traveling together it might be nice to have the congregation pray for the pilgrims before and during the trip. A custom in some places is to have the pastor pray over the travelers and pronounce a blessing. These steps tend to involve the entire community in the pilgrimage.

A related idea, popular in some churches, is to invite family, friends and members of the congregation to write out prayer petitions which the pilgrims then include in their group prayers at the holy places. Even if you are traveling alone, or are joining a less focused tour group, there is nothing stopping you from soliciting prayer petitions from family and friends. For many people back home it would be a thrill, and very edifying, to think that their family's needs are being included in prayers offered at the foot of Calvary or inside the cave at Bethlehem.

Scriptural Preparation

Everyone going on pilgrimage to the Holy Land ought to carry a Bible, preferably a small, light, paperback edition. In keeping with the times, some people might want to consider bringing one of the new electronic Franklin bibles. They are very small and include a concordance. Along with your Bible carry, if possible, a list of scripture citations appropriate for reading at the many holy sites. The Israeli Ministry of Tourism, Pilgrimage Promotion Division, distributes a free brochure entitled "Biblical Sites for Christian Visitors." This pamphlet briefly describes several dozen Old and New Testament sites with scripture citations, and would be very useful. It is available by writing to the Ministry at: P.O. Box 1018, Jerusalem, Israel, or at any of the eighteen Government Tourist Information offices in Israel, one of which is conveniently located near the Jaffa Gate in Jerusalem.

A more thorough pamphlet of the same type is available without charge from the Christian Information Center, located inside the Jaffa Gate, P.O. Box 14308, Jerusalem, Israel. It lists, for example, a dozen passages related to the Mount of Olives, seven concerning the Upper Room, ten dealing with Bethlehem, several on events which took place in the Judean Desert, all places you will visit. In addition to packing a Bible and an index to appropriate passages, it is strongly recommended that one sit down and read one of the Gospels, perhaps Matthew, in order to refresh one's memory of the sequence of events in Jesus' life. This could be done as a Bible study group.

VIDEOTAPES

There are a number of inspirational videotapes available which could profitably be viewed by individuals or groups preparing for a pilgrimage. Each has its special appeal. "Where Jesus Walked," is produced by United Christian Production Incorporated and distributed by Questar Video Incorporated, P.O. Box 11345, Chicago, Illinois 60611. Accompanied by a scriptural narrative and a musical score, the camera takes the viewer to all of the great shrines over the traditional sites of events in Christ's life. This video is a masterpiece and would appeal to both Catholics and a broad range of Protestants. The Moody Church in Chicago was involved in the project.

Another video recommended is "Israel, O Blessed Israel!" a gospel musical journey in the Holy Land featuring the narration and singing of Pat Boone. This is a stirring video tour of the towns, deserts and

mountainsides of Judea and Galilee. The camera spends little time at
the great Orthodox and Catholic shrines of antiquity, concentrating
rather on scenery, ruins, the Sea of Galilee, Masada, the Garden Tomb
and panoramic shots of the city of Jerusalem. Produced by John
Oronson and distributed by Palmer Distribution, Pauma Valley,
California 92061, it is successful in creating the urge to sing one's way
across the Holy Land. Pat's songs include "Israel, O Blessed Israel!,"
"Nearer My God to Thee," "I Walked Today Where Jesus Walked,"
"The Old Rugged Cross," "In the Garden," and "How Great Thou
Art."

"Steps Into the Holy Land" is a visual pilgrimage to the places of
Christ's life. Spectacular cinematography is accompanied by a fine narration in the sixty minute video, available for $19.95 from Vision
Video, P.O. Box 2249, Dept. 133, Livonia, Michigan 48151, tele-
phone 1-800-588-8474.

"A Walk With Jesus in the Holy Land" is available from Friends of
the Cross Communications, P.O. Box 1071, Grand Rapids, Michigan
49501, for a donation of $15.00 plus $2.00 postage and handling. This
sixty minute video follows the life of Christ from Nazareth to Calvary,
visiting most of the great shrines and holy sites in the life of Jesus, with
gospel readings and meditations led by Father Charles Antekeier, who
has led pilgrimages for a quarter century.

A more ambitious undertaking is the four hours of videocassettes
produced by Focus on the Family, under the title, "That the World May
Know." This series concentrates on the archeology, history and topography of the Old and New Testament sites and relates the material to the
study of the Bible.

Along with watching one of these inspirational videos, another good
idea is to study maps of the Holy Land, of modern Jerusalem, and of

the Old City. In addition to those included in this book, maps can be found in various books and articles, some referenced at the end of this book. The April 1996 *National Geographic* has outstanding maps of the Old City and Greater Jerusalem. Your enjoyment of any trip is enhanced by knowing where you are!

GETTING READY TO SING

One of the joys of group travel, especially on tour bus rides, is singing. What could be more enjoyable than passing the time on the road from Tel Aviv to Jerusalem singing songs about the Holy City or about the Lord or just about being a pilgrim? A perusal of any large hymn book will easily produce a number of songs which "fit" the scenes you will be visiting.

The *Lutheran Book of Worship* is a treasure trove of appropriate songs for a pilgrimage. For Bethlehem there are "Silent Night," "O Little Town of Bethlehem," and "Oh, Come All Ye Faithful." At the nearby Shepherd's Field, how about "The First Noel" and "Hark the Herald Angels Sing?" At the Jordan River baptismal site "Swing Low, Sweet Chariot" is appropriate. At Mount Tabor, the site of the Transfiguration you could sing, "How Good, Lord, to be Here."

Others in the same book, many of which will be found in books of other denominations, include "Were You There?" to be sung at Calvary, "Go to Dark Gethsemane" for a visit to the beautiful Church of All Nations, and "O Living Bread from Heaven" at the Upper Room. The list of perfect hymns for the holy places goes on and on. Many are fitting for the Upper Room, or Cenacle, on Mount Zion; others such as "Put Your Hand in the Hand" are naturals to be sung while crossing the Sea of Galilee.

"The Lord's Prayer," sung at the shrine commemorating it, the

Church of the Pater Noster on the Mount of Olives, has to be a unique experience. And how about "Jerusalem the Golden" or "Jerusalem Whose Towers Touch the Skies" as you look down at the Holy City from the Mount of Olives. "The Lord is my Shepherd" will raise consciousness as the bus hugs the side of a hill in Judea, perhaps passing a lone shepherd and a flock of sheep, a very common sight.

Two songs from the Lutheran book, which might serve as theme songs, are "Lord, as a Pilgrim" and "Rejoice, O Pilgrim Throng." An old Pentecostal hymnbook also has two candidates for theme songs: "I'm a Pilgrim" and "Jerusalem the Golden." A Presbyterian hymnal gives us two songs for a crossing of the Sea of Galilee: "Jesus Calls Us O'er the Tumult" and "Dear Lord and Father of Mankind." Then there is this favorite for time spent in the Galilean mountains: "How Lovely on the Mountains Are the Feet of Him."

A popular Catholic hymnbook entitled *Gather*, G.I.A. Publications, Chicago, 1994, is also a treasure trove of songs just made for singing in the Holy Land. Here are a few examples, just to get the reader going on your own church's hymnals: "Go Tell it on the Mountain" for Shepherd's Field, "Jerusalem, My Destiny" as a theme song for your pilgrimage, "At the Cross Her Station Keeping" and "Jesus, Remember Me" while walking on the Via Dolorosa (Way of the Cross), "Were You There?" at the chapel of Calvary, "Christ the Lord is Risen Today" when approaching the Holy Sepulchre, and "Come Holy Ghost" in the Upper Room. Three beauties for a visit to the Mount of Beatitudes: "Blest Are They," "Whatsoever You Do," and "We Are the Light of the World."

As churches have liberally borrowed each other's hymns over the last generation, many of these songs can be found in hymnals and songbooks of several denominations. Finally, if you can find a copy, there is a published book entitled, *Holy Land Singalong.*

THE WAY OF THE CROSS

If spirited congregational singing is a Lutheran gift to the church, the Way of the Cross is a precious contribution of Catholic origin. Everything about it should be theologically acceptable and aesthetically pleasing to Protestant and Orthodox pilgrims. People have been praying this prayer while walking the route of Jesus to his crucifixion since the fifth century. Although modern archeological discoveries suggest the traditional path through the Old City might not be the actual path followed by Jesus, the traditional route is hallowed by the very fact that for fifteen hundred years believers have prayed and wept their way along this route to Calvary.

For many it is the most moving experience of their pilgrimage. Hundreds walk it every day, some alone, some in pairs, some in small groups. During Holy Week thousands walk it. It is possible to obtain a cross to carry, allowing the pilgrim to literally share in Jesus' burden. When a group walks this route, known as the Via Dolorosa (Street of Sorrows), they take turns carrying the cross, which is not unduly heavy in any event.

There are fourteen stops, or stations, on the Way of the Cross. Most are scriptural, while a few are based on early Christian tradition. They begin with the condemnation of Jesus to death by Pilate and end with his being laid in the tomb. Each station is the occasion for a reading from scripture, group prayer and a reflection. Other Christians may be unaware that this form of meditation on the passion and death of Jesus Christ, which originated in Jerusalem, is practiced in Catholic churches all around the world. Most Catholic churches have fourteen paintings or sculptures, marking the Stations of the Cross, spaced along both side walls, allowing one to follow the Way of the Cross around the interior of the church building.

A beautifully illustrated, fold-out pamphlet to be used while walking and praying on the Via Dolorosa is widely available at shops in the Old City. Distributed by Mapline, P.O. Box 12262, Herzliya 46733, Israel, it is simply called "Via Dolorosa." Anyone attempting to make the Way of the Cross on the Via Dolorosa without a guide or group leader should most definitely obtain this little booklet, since it is easy to get turned around and difficult to locate some of the stations.

Most likely, the narrow streets will be filled with hawkers and shoppers, shoulder to shoulder, because the Old City is, among other things, an endless bazaar. This may be distracting, but imagine the scene on the fateful Friday in the year 30 A.D. Odds are the crowds carried on business as usual as Jesus struggled up and down the steep steps of the winding alleys of Jerusalem. You will be given no more deference by the crowds than he was.

Every Friday at 3:00 p.m. a group of Franciscans leads all who choose to participate in a mass procession along the Via Dolorosa, praying and singing in many different languages. To be part of this great public demonstration of love for Jesus and sorrow for sin is a peak experience for many pilgrims. One should be forewarned about the crowds at the Holy Sepulchre on Friday afternoons, however.

The stations have evolved over the centuries. Recently a few which were based on legend, like Veronica wiping Jesus' bloody face with her veil, have been replaced with commemoration of events more clearly based on the gospel narratives. A fifteenth station, celebrating the Resurrection, has become a popular addition in recent years. A few versions of the prayers, scripture readings and meditations available are *The Journey Continues, a Contemporary Way of the Cross*, available from Liguori Publications, One Liguori Drive, Liguori, Missouri 63057-9999; *The Biblical Way of the Cross*; and *Everyone's*

Way of the Cross, both available from Ave Maria Press, Notre Dame, Indiana 46556.

A fitting ending to this chapter is the following prayer by John M. Haffert. It might appeal to readers as the official group prayer for your pilgrimage. Pray it often before and during your visit to the Holy Land.

A Pilgrim's Prayer

If some things do not happen as they are scheduled, Lord, may I remember that I am a pilgrim not a tourist!

If I should get tired and inclined to become short-tempered, Lord, may I remember that I am a pilgrim not a tourist!

If my meal in a foreign country may not be to my particular liking, Lord, may I remember that I am a pilgrim not a tourist!

If any delays should occur and I should become anxious, Lord, may I remember that I am a pilgrim not a tourist!

If some other pilgrim is making noise so that I cannot hear the guide, Lord, may I remember that I am a pilgrim and not a tourist when I ask that person to be a bit more quiet!

If someone takes a better seat or more choice place, Lord, may I remember that I am a pilgrim not a tourist!

If I find myself last in line waiting, Lord, may I remember that I am a pilgrim not a tourist!

If the person in front of me buys the last item which I really wanted, Lord, may I remember that I am a pilgrim not a tourist!

If I should get a chance to help another person, who always seems to be annoying me, Lord, may I remember that I am a pilgrim not a tourist!

If someone is always the "last one on the bus" and I am always on time, Lord, may I remember that I am a pilgrim not a tourist!

But Lord, especially let me remember that what I find objectionable in another is really what You oftentimes find objectionable in me and let me remember this and forgive the other, as You are continually forgiving me!

15.

Picking The Right Tour

TOURISTS AND PILGRIMS

People travel to Israel for many reasons. It is, of course, the goal of the world's Jews to see the ancient places associated with their religion and history, but also to experience modern Jewish society in the State of Israel. The enthusiastic clapping of Jewish passengers when their plane lands at Ben-Gurion Airport conveys a little of the pride Jews feel in the nation-building miracles achieved in a mere half century.

For many visitors, both Jews and others, the attractions include the semi tropical resort town of Eilat, Israel's spa and diving resort on the Red Sea. The Mediterranean Sea beaches of Tel Aviv appeal to those simply on vacation. Both Tel Aviv and Jerusalem have lavish high-rise hotels catering to affluent travelers, not to mention resort

Camel riding; a great photo opportunity.

hotels in Haifa on the Mediterranean and Tiberias on the Sea of Galilee. A stay at a kibbutz, skiing on Mount Hermon, an archeological dig or jeep trek in the Negev Desert are also possible. Overland extensions to neighboring Jordan and Egypt can add further adventure.

A promotional pamphlet published by the Ministry of Tourism trumpets this multifaceted industry:

> There are so many reasons why people are attracted to Israel. For some, it's the sun-drenched climate. For others, it's the rich variety of sites and sights—historical, archeological, religious or just beautiful. For still others, it's the fascinating contrast between the ancient and the modern.

It is easy to see that a pilgrim has to be careful not to end up on an inappropriate tour. Scuba diving at Eilat and life on a kibbutz sound like fun, but are not the stuff of which Christian pilgrimages are made.

Of course, you may be traveling with a church group, in which case you are hopefully assured of a spiritually-oriented trip. Even then, there are things you can do to enhance the planned trip for everyone concerned. If, on the other hand, you are picking a tour from a newspaper ad or on the recommendation of your travel agent, there is much you need to consider. Tour leaders, including church leaders, can influence a tour if they are willing to be pro-active. Overseas travel agencies and tour companies contract with local tour companies in Israel, which in turn employ the local guides and set the itineraries. Details can be modified at the insistence of the spiritual leaders of the group, but, as one experienced clergyman has said: "Many travel agencies give you the impression the tour guide is in charge, but he is not. He is only an employee hired by the agency. The clergy leading the pilgrimage should act as such, but they have to have done their homework before the trip."

ONE GROUP'S ADVICE

A critique done by one group from Grand Rapids, Michigan, after returning from a pilgrimage is revealing and helpful. These were some of their criticisms and suggestions for future tours:

1. Provide more time for prayer and meditation at special places, such as the Mount of the Beatitudes, Mount Tabor and Gethsemane.
2. Don't take too large a group. Keep it manageable.
3. Reduce the number of stops at souvenir shops, carpet shops, diamond factories and other commercial places.

4. Arrange for a regular daily period of group prayer, perhaps on the bus.

5. Regular group singing of hymns and also of popular songs.

6. Shorten lunch stops.

7. Provide an opportunity to visit the Knesset (parliament building in Jerusalem), the Hebrew University, the Holocaust Memorial and a modern shopping district in West Jerusalem.

Under the heading of things in their pilgrimage they would not want to change, these pilgrims compiled the following thoughtful list:

1. Living in the Old City at a pilgrim hospice.

2. Time spent at the Holy Sepulchre.

3. Visit with a patriarch and Eastern clergy.

4. Worship at a different holy place each day.

5. Visit with Father Elias Chacour. (See Chapter 13.)

6. Crossing the Sea of Galilee.

7. Being in the Upper Room.

8. Renewal of baptismal vows in the Jordan River.

9. Taking turns carrying the cross on the Via Dolorosa.

One of the more intriguing proposals coming out of the critique was that a future pilgrimage include an all-day retreat at the Mount of Beatitudes overlooking the Sea of Galilee, the place Jesus chose for his Sermon on the Mount. Every standard tour itinerary could benefit by spending more time in this region of Galilee.

MAKING TIME FOR PRAYER

As you can see, there is room for improvement in the fairly standard itineraries now in vogue in the Holy Land. One obstacle is commented on by a guide interviewed by Father Wild: "Tours are not for praying, they're for making money." Yes, the profit motive is present

A tropical garden at the Mount of the Beatitudes along the Sea of Galilee.

everywhere, even in the travel business. That is understandable, even necessary, but it need not control the itinerary your group chooses. The travel industry wants to please you, the customer.

Father Wild has some words of wisdom for planners:

> Somehow the spirit of pilgrimage has been sold out to the guides and the tourist agencies. Do these people on tours want more time to pray and linger? If so, why don't they inform the guides of their intentions? The people pay the money. Why can't they pray for an hour in each of the holy places? In an attempt to 'get everything in,' hundreds of thousands of people are rushed through the shrines like crowds going through turnstiles at a football stadium....
>
> People who arrange the tours should make it clear to the agencies what it is they want. Surely they should want quality on a pilgrimage,

Mountainous backdrop of the Dead Sea.

not quantity. See fewer places and pray more. Don't rush through these sacred places as if you're touring a museum. Prayer and time for reflection are everything on a pilgrimage.

ITINERARIES

The people organizing a pilgrimage need to decide what kind of mix they wish, such as visiting Gospel holy places, spending time in the countryside, visiting Old Testament holy sites, and experiencing contemporary Jewish and Arab life. Hopefully there will be opportunities for all of the above.

In addition to spending time at many of the holy places in the Jerusalem area and in Galilee, most Christian-oriented tours visit the Arab city of Jericho, the Jewish resort city of Tiberias (a convenient base from which to visit all of Galilee) and the coastal city of Haifa. A visit to

Applying a therapeutic mudpack before entering the Dead Sea for a float.

Haifa should include a stop at the gorgeous building and grounds of the Bahai Temple, the cave of the Prophet Elijah and the foundation monastery of the worldwide Carmelite Order, built during the Crusades on the top of Mount Carmel overlooking the Mediterranean.

A day trip from Jerusalem to Qumran to see the caves where the Dead Sea Scrolls were found is standard fare, along with the fun of floating in the saline water of the Dead Sea, the lowest spot on earth. This is a relaxing day off from the intensely spiritual itinerary and is a time for play. If the excursion along the Dead Sea is a full day, it may include a cable car ride to the mountaintop fortress of Masada, made famous by the brave Jewish defenders against the Roman army nineteen hundred years ago.

One recommendation this author would make is that Protestant-sponsored tours spend more time in prayer and reflection at the momentous and historic shrines over the holy places, and that the typical Catholic or Orthodox tours spend more time out in the countryside made holy by Jesus' presence.

Virtually all tours visit the Western Wall and the Muslim shrines on the Temple Mount, and that is as it should be. A visit to at least one Palestinian Christian community should become standard, perhaps including an opportunity to pray with the people and to mix socially. This would require some planning, but is possible. The Greek Orthodox, Greek Catholic, Syrian Orthodox and Latin church offices in the Old City should be contacted in this regard. The Ecumenical Travel Office of the Middle East Council of Churches has pioneered tours integrating visits to traditional holy sites with exposure to the lives of the Christian people living in the area. Father Chacour's Prophet Elias College in Ibellin, Galilee, mentioned earlier, is one place where pilgrims, individuals or groups, can actually pitch in and work on construction projects, demonstrating solidarity with the local church. Group tours of the college are also available. Fax inquiries to 04-9869573. Both the Notre Dame Center and the Swedish Christian Study Center can assist in connecting groups with local church leaders and congregations. The latter prepares itineraries for visiting groups who want to meet with local Christians, Jews and Muslims. It can be contacted at: P.O. Box 14233, Jerusalem, 91141, Israel. Another source of help at the Jaffa Gate area is the Christian Information Center, P.O. Box 14308, Jerusalem, Israel.

HOSPICES

The Holy Land suffers from a shortage of accommodations aimed at the specific needs of pilgrims. The majority of organized Christian tours stay at first class commercial hotels featuring some of the most lavish buffets you will ever see. While everyone needs a comfortable bed in a pleasant room, a first class hotel where most of the guests are living the dolce vita is not the best ambiance for a pilgrimage to our spiritual roots. The limited number of pilgrim hospices may well be due to the assumption by the local tour agencies that Westerners, even pilgrims, demand these luxuries. Is that true?

This writer has found the church-sponsored hospices he has stayed at or visited to be places of comfort and warmth and cultural interest. Perhaps the largest is Notre Dame of Jerusalem Center, just outside the New Gate of the Old City. The staff includes Palestinian, Armenian, African and other Christian lay people, while the guests are from all over the world, including pilgrims, students and scholars. It is also an ecumenical and pastoral center for Jerusalem Christians of all church communities, creating another opportunity for meeting native believers. The Center has numerous forms of outreach to the Christians of the Holy Land. Pilgrims may join its Association of Friends, which can be contacted at: P.O. Box 20531, Jerusalem.

Another very interesting pilgrim house is attached to the Greek (Melkite) Catholic Patriarchate in the Old City. This eighty-six bed hospice offers pilgrims the unique opportunity to have contact with a Byzantine Rite church, meet its people and participate in its beautiful liturgy.

The Franciscans operate pilgrim hospices under the name Casa Nova in the Old City, in Bethlehem and in Nazareth. These are all well established and open to all pilgrims. Others are the Christ Church Hospice (Anglican), St. George's Cathedral Hostel (Anglican), the Franciscan White Sisters of Mary Hospice, St. Andrew's Guest House (Church of Scotland), and the YMCA Aelia Capitolina, all in or close to the Old City.

Christian hospices are listed and described, with addresses, in a paperback book published by the Ministry of Tourism under the name *Pilgrims and Christian Tourists Promotion Handbook*, available from the Israel Government Tourist Office, 5 South Wabash Avenue, Chicago, Illinois 60603-3073, phone 312-782-4306 or 800-782-4306. Forty-three in number, they are mostly small and sponsored by a variety of churches, including Baptist, Anglican, Roman Catholic, Armenian Catholic, Lutheran, Greek Catholic, Orthodox, Church of Scotland, Syrian Catholic, Maronite, Evangelical, and the nondenominational YMCA. Two hospices which sound intriguing by virtue of their privileged locations are the Franciscan Convent of the Transfiguration on top of Mount Tabor and the Ospizio Sul Monte della Beatitudine at the Mount of the Beatitudes along the Sea of Galilee. Just imagine staying overnight in the stillness of such 0sanctified space.

GUIDES

A few thousand people are licensed by the Israeli government as guides, of whom only a handful are Christian Arabs. Although the Jewish guides and the few Muslim guides are very knowledgeable about the gospel stories and the Christian holy places, there is something fitting about being led by a Christian guide who identifies with the Gospel events being described. For the most part, the government requires tours to be in the hands of its licensed guides. Of course a knowledgeable pastor may supplement the guide's explanations as he pleases. And, as might be expected in a country racked by fifty years of ethnic hostility, guides may portray the Israeli-Palestinian conflict according to their personal prejudices. As it happens, most guides are Jewish. This point is made by Bowman in his

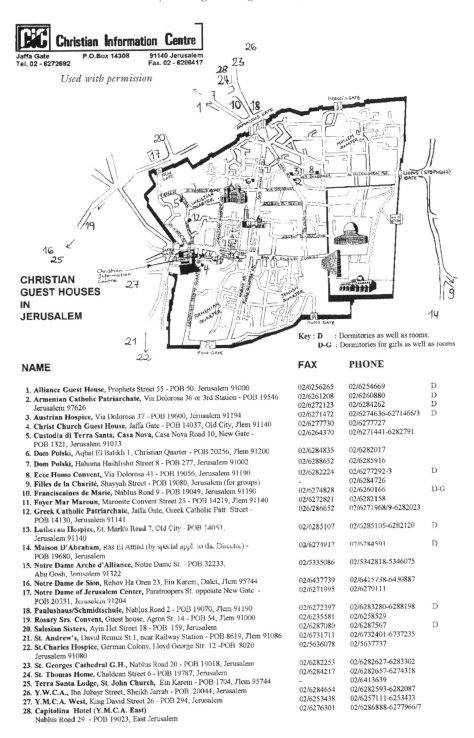

Christian Information Centre

Jaffa Gate   P.O.Box 14308   91140 Jerusalem
Tel. 02 - 6272692   Fax. 02 - 6286417

Used with permission

**CHRISTIAN
GUEST HOUSES
IN
JERUSALEM**

Key : **D**   : Dormitories as well as rooms.
       D-G : Dormitories for girls as well as rooms

NAME	FAX	PHONE	
1. **Alliance Guest House**, Prophets Street 55 - POB 50, Jerusalem 91000	02/6256265	02/6254669	D
2. **Armenian Catholic Patriarchate**, Via Dolorosa 36 or 3rd Station - POB 19546 Jerusalem 97626	02/6261208 02/6272123	02/6260880 02/6284262	D D
3. **Austrian Hospice**, Via Dolorosa 37 - POB 19600, Jerusalem 91194	02/6271472	02/6274636-6271466/3	D
4. **Christ Church Guest House**, Jaffa Gate - POB 14037, Old City, J'lem 91140	02/6277730	02/6277727	
5. **Custodia di Terra Santa, Casa Nova**, Casa Nova Road 10, New Gate - POB 1321, Jerusalem 91013	02/6264370	02/6271441-6282791	
6. **Dom Polski**, Aqbat El Batikh 1, Christian Quarter - POB 20256, J'lem 91200	02/6284835	02/6282017	
7. **Dom Polski**, Hahoma Hashlishit Street 8 - POB 277, Jerusalem 91002	02/6288652	02/6285916	
8. **Ecce Homo Convent**, Via Dolorosa 41 - POB 19056, Jerusalem 91190	02/6282224	02/6277292-3	D
9. **Filles de la Charité**, Shayyah Street - POB 19080, Jerusalem (for groups)	-	02/6284726	
10. **Franciscaines de Marie**, Nablus Road 9 - POB 19049, Jerusalem 91190	02/6274828	02/6260166	D-G
11. **Foyer Mar Maroun**, Maronite Convent Street 25 - POB 14219, J'lem 91140	02/6272821	02/6282158	
12. **Greek Catholic Patriarchate**, Jaffa Gate, Greek Catholic Patr. Street - POB 14130, Jerusalem 91141	026/286652	02/6271968/9-6282023	
13. **Lutheran Hospice**, St. Mark's Road 7, Old City - POB 14051, Jerusalem 91140	02/6285107	02/6285105-6282120	D
14. **Maison D'Abraham**, Ras El Amud (by special appl. to the Director) - POB 19680, Jerusalem	02/6274917	02/6784591	D
15. **Notre Dame Arche d'Alliance**, Notre Dame St. - POB 32233, Abu Gosh, Jerusalem 91322	02/5335086	02/5342818-5346075	
16. **Notre Dame de Sion**, Rehov Ha Oren 23, Ein Karem, Dalet, J'lem 95744	02/6437739	02/6415738-6430887	
17. **Notre Dame of Jerusalem Center**, Paratroopers St. opposite New Gate - POB 20531, Jerusalem 91204	02/6271995	02/6279111	
18. **Paulushaus/Schmidtschule**, Nablus Road 2 - POB 19070, J'lem 91190	02/6272397	02/6283280-6288198	D
19. **Rosary Srs. Convent**, Guest house, Agron St. 14 - POB 54, J'lem 91000	02/6235581	02/6258529	
20. **Salesian Sisters**, Ayin Het Street 18 - POB 159, Jerusalem	02/6287080	02/6287567	D
21. **St. Andrew's**, David Remez St.1, near Railway Station - POB 8619, J'lem 91086	02/6731711	02/6732401-6737235	
22. **St. Charles Hospice**, German Colony, Lloyd George Str. 12 -POB 8020 Jerusalem 91080	02/5636078	02/5637737	
23. **St. Georges Cathedral G.H.**, Nablus Road 20 - POB 19018, Jerusalem	02/6282253	02/6282627-6283302	
24. **St. Thomas Home**, Chaldean Street 6 - POB 19787, Jerusalem	02/6284217	02/6282657-6274318	
25. **Terra Santa Lodge, St. John Church**, Ein Karem - POB 1704, J'lem 95744	-	02/6413639	
26. **Y.W.C.A.**, Ibn Jubayr Street, Sheikh Jarrah - POB 20044, Jerusalem	02/6284654	02/6282593-6282087	
27. **Y.M.C.A. West**, King David Street 26 - POB 294, Jerusalem	02/6253438	02/6257111-6253433	
28. **Capitolina Hotel (Y.M.C.A. East)** Nablus Road 29 - POB 19023, East Jerusalem	02/6276301	02/6286888-6277966/7	

study of tour guides in the Holy Land, included in the bibliography. Because assessments of the Arab-Israeli conflict tend to be so polarized, depending upon the source, one is cautioned to evaluate opinions with a degree of skepticism. Draw your own conclusions.

16.

Now For A Little Fun

The answers to the quizzes which follow can be found somewhere in this book. Your success will show you are ready for a pilgrimage. If you miss more than half, perhaps you should reread the book! The correct answers follow the last quiz. Have fun. Remember, a pilgrimage should be enjoyable as well as inspiring. The two are not mutually exclusive.

The author coming out of Lazarus' tomb. We needed a little levity after a long day of visiting holy places.

Match the Dates to their Mates

1. 1900 B.C.	(a) King Solomon builds first temple.
2. 1250 B.C.	(b) Apostolic Age; New Testament written.
3. 1000 B.C.	(c) First temple destroyed; exile in Babylon.
4. 960 B.C.	(d) King Herod builds the second temple.
5. 587 B.C.	(e) Era of the Patriarchs Abraham, Isaac and Jacob.
6. 20 B.C.	(f) Crucifixion and resurrection of Jesus Christ.
7. 4 B.C.	(g) Roman army destroys the second temple.
8. 30 A.D.	(h) Exodus from Egypt led by Moses.
9. 30-100 A.D.	(i) The Incarnation of Jesus Christ.
10. 70 A.D.	(j) King David makes Jerusalem his capital.
11. 135 A.D.	(k) Bar Kochba revolt. Romans rebuild Jerusalem as Aelia Capitolina; Jewish dispersion (diaspora) begins.

True or False

Circle the correct answer to the statements below.

1. References to the Latins, or the Latin Church, mean the Roman Catholic Church. T F

2. Calvary was outside the city walls in 30 A.D. and is inside today. T F

3. The Upper Room once held the Ark of the Covenant. T F

4. The Dead Sea Scrolls were found in Tel Aviv. T F

5. The greatest concentration of Holy Land native Christians is in Galilee. T F

6. Most Christian visitors to the Holy Land stay in religious hospices. T   F

What Happened on Which Mountain?

1. Mount Scopus	(a) Elijah's cave. Foundation of Carmelite Order
2. Mount Hermon	(b) Site of Jesus' greatest recorded preaching
3. Mount Carmel	(c) Ten Commandments given to Moses by God
4. Mount of Olives	(d) City of David. Upper Room. Dormition Abbey
5. Mount Sinai	(e) Jewish cemeteries. Yad Vashem Holocaust Memorial
6. Mount Tabor	(f) A misnomer. Only a slight elevation
7. Mount Zion	(g) Hebrew University of Jerusalem
8. Mount Herzl	(h) Dome of the Rock and al Aksa Mosque
9. Mount Calvary	(i) Where Crusaders met their downfall
10. Temple Mount	(j) Israeli ski resorts
11. Mount of Beatitudes	(k) Where Jesus withdrew to pray
12. Horns of Hattin	(l) Transfiguration of Jesus, with Moses and Elijah

Multiple Choice

Choose the best answer.

1.   Pilgrimage _____.

a.   is a uniquely Christian phenomenon.

b.   reached a fever pitch between 900 A.D. and 1100 A.D.

c.   is still a risky business.

d.   is a form of tourism.

e.   is not encouraged by the government of Israel.

2.   The Latin Kingdom of Jerusalem _____.

a.   lasted from 1100-1187 A.D.

b.   made alliances with Muslim nations.

c.   rebuilt Jerusalem and the Holy Land with great churches and castles.

d.   was founded by the heroic Godfrey de Bouillon.

e.   all of the above.

Match More Dates to Mates

1. 313 A.D.   (a) Greatest era of Christian pilgrimage, much of it on foot.

2. 325 A.D.   (b) First Crusade captures Jerusalem. Christian kingdom established.

3. 636 A.D.   (c) British Mandate government.

4. 900-1100 A.D.   (d) Two centuries of Crusader civilization ends. Saint John of Acre falls.

5. 1010 A.D.   (e) Empress Helena builds shrines over holy places.

6. 1099 A.D.   (f) Turkish rule. Churches struggle for survival.

7. 1187 A.D.   (g) Six-Day War. Israel occupies West Bank, Sinai, etc.

8. 1291 A.D.   (h) Edict of Milan. Emperor Constantine liberates Christian religion. Three centuries of Christian Palestine begin.

9. 1300-1900 A.D.   (i) State of Israel.

10. 1917-1948 A.D.   (j) Mad Caliph al-Hakim desecrates Holy Sepulchre.

11. 1948-present   (k) Saladin retakes Jerusalem. Crusaders retreat to coastal cities.

12. 1967 A.D.   (l) Mohammed's new religion conquers Christian Palestine.

"Rat" Facts-Did You Know?

- General Gordon saw Calvary and the empty tomb in a dream and was led to what is now the Garden Tomb.

- The Mamelukes, who ruled Palestine before and after the Crusades, had been Egyptian slaves.

- The Persians, when destroying Byzantine Christian churches, including the Holy Sepulchre, in 614 A.D., spared the Church of the Nativity in Bethlehem because of icons of the Magi who resembled Persian wise men.

- Bethlehem, today, is almost a suburb of Jerusalem.

- The leaders of the ancient Christian denominations in the Holy Land are now meeting together on a regular basis for the first time.

- The Greek Catholics of the Holy Land are also called Melkites (king's men) because their ancestors were loyal to the Patriarch of Constantinople, and therefore to the Byzantine Emperor, during the Fifth Century controversy over the two natures of Christ (divine and human). The Syrian (Jacobite) Church, Egyptian (Coptic) Church and Armenian Church rejected the doctrine taught at the Council of Chalcedon, and defied the will of the Byzantine church and emperor.

- The Knights Templar and Knights of Saint John, founded in the Holy Land during the Crusades, still exist in modified form, and the Equestrian Order of the Knights of the Holy Sepulchre has been revived as an international support group for the work of the church in the Holy Land.

- There are far more Christian Palestinians in America than in the Holy Land. Many have settled in the suburbs of Detroit.

- You have to stoop to enter both the Church of the Nativity in Bethlehem and the tomb of Christ inside the Church of the Holy Sepulchre. It is said that the unusually low doorway in Bethlehem was designed to keep invading armies from entering on horseback.

- During the 500s A.D., the golden age of the Byzantine Holy Land, as many as three thousand Christian holy men lived as hermits in the Judean Desert at any given time.

- Israel's celebration of Jerusalem 3000 in 1996 marked the anniversary of David's conquest of the Jebusite city, making it Israel's capital.

Match Each With Something That Replaced it
or Has Stood in The Same Place:

1. Jerusalem

2. Calvary-the-Cross

3. The Temple

4. Mount Sinai

5. Temple Mount

6. David's Tomb

7. Christ's Empty Tomb

8. Elijah's Cave

9. Tombs of the Patriarchs

10. Place where Jesus was tried

11. Marriage feast of Cana

12. King Herod's Citadel

13. Site of the Martyrdom of Apostle James, first bishop of Jerusalem

14. Jesus' route carrying the cross

15. First Christian martyr killed here

16. Gethsemane

17. Post-resurrection appearance of Jesus to disciples on shore of Sea of Galilee

a. First Carmelite Monastery

b. The Upper Room, or Cenacle

c. Shrine to Roman god Jupiter

d. Roman statue of Venus

e. Dome of the Rock

f. Monastery of Saint Catherine

g. Haram al-Sharif

h. Aelia Capitolina

i. Galilean town of Kefer Kanna

j. Mosque in Hebron

k. Church of Saint Peter in Gallicantu (Cock Crowed)

l. The Via Dolorosa

m. Museum of the City of Jerusalem

n. Church of All Nations (or Church of the Agony)

o. Church of the Primacy of Peter

p. Armenian Cathedral in Old City

q. Saint Stephen's Gate

Countries Bordering Israel: True or False?

1. France   T F

2. Lebanon   T F

3. Syria   T F

4. Saudi Arabia   T F

5. Egypt   T F

6. Jordan   T F

7. Iraq   T F

Match the Gates of Jerusalem

1. Zion Gate
2. Damascus Gate

3. New Gate

4. Jaffa Gate

5. Dung Gate

6. Herod's Gate

7. Golden (Heavenly) Gate

8. Lion (Saint Stephen's) Gate

a. Entrance from the north
b. Main entrance to Christian Quarter
c. Entrance to Armenian and Jewish Quarter
d. Main entrance to Jewish Quarter
e. Main entrance from East Jerusalem
f. Messiah prophesied to enter city through it
g. Near Notre Dame Center and Latin Patriarchate
h. Where Jesus' passion began

Protestant, Orthodox and Catholic Pilgrimage Symbols

Match them up:

1. Protestant

2. Orthodox

3. Catholic

a. Via Dolorosa

b. The Garden Tomb

c. Ceremony of the Holy Fire

d. Praying in the Countryside

e. Preparation for a happy death

f. Moving from holy place to holy place

Pick One Answer:

1. Sephardim ____:

a. is the branch of Judaism which used to speak Ladino

b. was the last Christian Patriarch before Muslim conquest

c. defeated Crusaders at the Horns of Hattin

2. The Coptic Church ____:

a. has a little monastery on the roof of the Holy Sepulchre

b. has its own quarter in the Old City of Jerusalem

c. maintains a small shrine at the back of the tomb of Christ

3. The Custody of the Holy Land refers to____:

a. British rule from 1917-1947 A.D.

b. the Franciscan organization which has maintained most
   Catholic shrines for 700 years

c. the oppressive Turkish rule from 1300-1900 A.D.

4. The Crusader king who tried to make peace with the Muslims was ____:

a. Saint Louis IX of France

b. Richard the Lion Heart of England

c. King Baldwin I of Jerusalem

d. Kaiser Wilhelm of Prussia

e. Byzantine Emperor Justinian

f. Saint Francis of Assisi

5. The International Christian Embassy ___:

a. negotiated a peace treaty with Saladin.

b. is a Christian Zionist organization which sponsors mass assemblies in Jerusalem.

c. promotes unity among Christian communities in the Holy Land.

d. promotes Christian-Muslim harmony.

e. both (c) and (d).

THE ANSWERS

Match the Dates to their Mates

1. e		7. i	
2. h		8. f	
3. j		9. b	
4. a		10. g	
5. c		11. k	
6. d			

True or False

1. T	4. F
2. T	5. T
3. F	6. F

What Happened on Which Mountain?

1. g	7. d
2. j	8. e
3. a	9. f
4. k	10. h
5. c	11. b
6. l	12. i

Multiple Choice-Choose the best answer

Pilgrimage: b

The Latin Kingdom of Jerusalem: e

Match More Dates to Mates

1. h	7. k
2. e	8. d
3. l	9. f
4. a	10. c
5. j	11. i
6. b	12. g

"Rat" Facts-All Are True

Match each with something that replaced it or has stood in the same place.

1. h	10. k
2. d	11. i
3. e	12. m
4. f	13. p
5. g	14. l
6. b	15. q
7. c	16. n
8. a	17. o
9. j	

Countries Bordering Israel: True or False?

1. F   4. F

2. T   5. T

3. T   6. T

                        7. F

Match the Gates of Jerusalem

1. d   5. c

2. e   6. a

3. g   7. f

4. b   8. h

Protestant, Orthodox and Catholic Pilgrimage Symbols

1. b and d

2. c and e

3. a and f

Pick One Answer

1. Sephardim: a

2. Coptic Church: c

3. The Custody of the Holy Land: b

4. Crusader king who tried to make peace with the Muslims: b

5. The International Christian Embassy: b

Epilogue

When Marilyn and I were approaching our twenty-fifth wedding anniversary we decided to celebrate by taking a trip. Just for fun we asked ourselves where we would go if we had the privilege of traveling anywhere in the world but had only one trip left in our lives.

We briefly toyed with the major areas we had not seen, such places as China, Russia and Australia. The idea of a pilgrimage to the Holy Land somehow came to the fore. We quickly settled on this as the mother of all trips for any serious Christian believer.

I don't know why we had never considered it before. Perhaps we grow up thinking of the Holy Land as a state of mind, a place which existed long ago and far away, something like Camelot, inaccessible except through the imagination.

*Church of All Nations, built over the rocky area believed to be the place
where Jesus prayed at Gethsemane the night before the crucifixion.*

Several years as a Bible study leader had unconsciously whetted my
appetite for the places where Jesus spent his earthly life. The more I
thought about it, the more I wondered how I could even have considered other choices. Fortunately my enthusiasm was infectious and
Marilyn agreed. We traveled that summer both independently and with
a tour group selected from a magazine ad.

Upon our return home from that first pilgrimage, I wanted to share
my enthusiasm with as many people as possible. Continuing to read
everything I could get my hands on, I began to see that such a trip can
be more than a brief time warp. It has potential for promoting community among the divergent branches of the church which, after all, worship the one God, Father, Son and Spirit.

I felt led to make a small contribution to Christian unity by writing

a self-consciously ecumenical book about the Holy Land, one not written exclusively from an Evangelical or Catholic or Lutheran or other
faith perspective. Given my feelings about the urgency of reestablishing
Christian unity in some form as a sign to the world, the task was a congenial one.

Experiences during a later trip to do research for this book, living
at a hospice run by one of the native Arab churches, opened my eyes
to another crying need, solidarity with these descendants of the first
Christian community. The more I observed them and studied their
fascinating history, the more I wanted to make Western Christians
aware of them and their needs. Hopefully this has been achieved to
some degree.

In the course of traveling through the Holy Land, with two very different Christian tour groups, I have learned much from my fellow travelers. They have truly been "pilgrims, not tourists." Their ebullience in
the face of heat and sore feet has convinced me that there are millions
of Christians who could and should make this trip of a lifetime.

I have also learned from cohorts that there is a crying need for historical background before leaving home. That means Bible history and
the history of people, places and events in the Holy Land since the time
of Christ.

So armed, we see all the layers when we enter an Eastern Christian
church or an historic mosque or synagogue, or meet an Arab merchant
or a young Israeli soldier. Since so many speak English we can actually
befriend these people across the cultural and religious divides.
Understanding their sincerely held beliefs, we will naturally be more
sensitive to their feelings, thereby making a small contribution to mutual understanding.

Two thousand years after the birth of Jesus we look forward to the dawn of a new day in the Holy Land, one in which Jews and Arabs, both Muslim and Christian, will live in peace; and one in which Christian churches, with age-old rights to custody of the holy places, will generously extend the privilege of formal worship services to other communities, sharing as sisters and brothers in the Lord.

We pilgrims can at least do our part to make it a place where "they," meaning the unbelieving world, "will know we are Christians by our love." For us, the land made holy by the life of Christ is our spiritual homeland on earth. Traveling there is a Christian family reunion. At such times families set aside differences and celebrate what they have in common. Let us go and do likewise.

Bibliography

Awwad, Sami. *The Holy Land in Colour*. Jerusalem: Golden Press, 1993.

Bacon, Isabelle. *Walking Beside Jesus in the Holy Land*. Amana Books, 1992.

Bowman, Glenn. "Christian Ideology and the Image of a Holy Land: The Place of Jerusalem Pilgrimage in the Various Christianities." *Contesting the Sacred: The Anthropology of Christian Pilgrimage*. London: Greenwood Press, 1991 (98-121).

Bowman, Glenn. "Nationalising the Sacred: Shrines and Shifting Identities in the Israeli-Occupied Territories." *Man: Journal of the Royal Anthropological Association*. XXVIII:3, Sept. 1993 (431-460).

Bowman, Glenn. "Pilgrim Narratives and their Object: A Study in Ideological Distortion." *Sacred Journeys: The Anthropology of Pilgrimage*. London: Greenwood Press, 1992 (149-168).

Bowman, Glenn. "The Politics of Tour Guiding: Israeli and Palestinian Guides in Israel and the Occupied Territories," in David Harrison ed. *Tourism and the Less-Developed Countries.* London: 1991 (121-134).

Burge, Gary M. *Who Are God's People in the Middle East?* Grand Rapids: Zondervan, 1993.

Chacour, Elias with David Hazard. *Blood Brothers.* Old Tappan, New Jersey: Fleming H. Revell Co., 1984.

Chammas, Joseph. *The Melkite Church.* Jerusalem, 1992.

Coleman, Simon and John Elsner. *Pilgrimage: Past and Present in the World Religions.* Harvard University Press, 1995.

Cragg, Kenneth. *The Arab Christian, A History in the Middle East.* Louisville: Westminster-John Knox Press, 1991.

Custody of the Holy Land. Author Anonymous. Jerusalem: Franciscan Printing Press, 1981.

Descy, Serge. *The Melkite Church.* Newton: Sophia Press, 1993.

Doyle, Stephen. *The Pilgrim's New Guide to the Holy Land.* Collegeville, MN: Liturgical Press, 1985.

Elon, Amos. *Jerusalem: City of Mirrors.* Boston: Little Brown, 1989.

Erdmann, Carl. *The Origin of the Idea of Crusade.* Stuttgart, 1935. English trans. Princeton: Princeton University Press, 1977.

Freeman-Grenville, G.S.P. *The Holy Land: A Pilgrim's Guide to Israel, Jordan, and the Sinai.* New York: Continuum, 1996.

Friedman, Thomas L. *From Beirut to Jerusalem.* New York: Doubleday, 1989.

Fulcher of Chartres. *A History of the Expedition to Jerusalem, 1095-1127.* Knoxville: University of Tennessee Press, 1969.

Gillingham, John. *Richard the Lionheart.* New York: Times Books, 1978.

Girzone, Joseph F. *Joshua in the Holy Land.* New York: Simon & Schuster, 1992.

Graham, Stephan. *With the Russian Pilgrims to Jerusalem*. London, 1913.

Hoade, Eugene. *Guide to the Holy Land*. Jerusalem: Franciscan Printing Press, 1971.

Hoade, Eugene. *Western Pilgrims*. Jerusalem: Franciscan Printing Press, 1952.

In the Footsteps of the Master. Nashville: Ideals Publishing Corp., 1991.

Jerusalem: The Diocesan Bulletin of the Latin Patriarchate. Jan.-Feb., 1995.

Kilgallen, John J. *A New Testament Guide to the Holy Land*. Chicago: Loyola University Press, 1987.

Kollek, Teddy. *Next Year in Jerusalem*. Harvest House Publishers, 1995.

"The Melkites of Jerusalem." *Catholic Near East*. 21:6, Nov.-Dec., 1995.

Michener, James A. *The Source*. New York: Random House, 1965.

Munro, Dana Carlton. *The Kingdom of the Crusaders*. D. Appleton Century Co., 1935.

Murphy-O'Connor, Jerome. *The Holy Land: An Archeological Guide*. Oxford University Press, 1980, 1992.

O'Mahony, Anthony, editor with Goran Gunner and Kevork Hintlian. *The Christian Heritage in the Holy Land*. London: Scorpion Cavendish, 1995.

Peters, Edward, ed. *The First Crusade, the Chronicle of Fulcher of Chartres and Other Source Materials*. Philadelphia: University of Pennsylvania Press, 1971.

"Pilgrimage." *Encyclopedia of Religion and Ethics*. vol. 10.

Prior, Michael and William Taylor, editors. *Christians in the Holy Land*. London: World of Islam Festival Trust, 1994.

Rafael, Nicholas. *Come and See: Holy Land Pilgrimage Guidebook for Orthodox Christians*. Jamestown, New York, 1995.

Raya, Joseph. *Byzantine Church and Culture.* Allendale, New Jersey: Alleluia Press, 1992.

"Retracing the First Crusade." *National Geographic.* Sept. 1989.

Rock, Albert. *The Status Quo in the Holy Places.* Jerusalem: Franciscan Printing Press, 1989.

Runciman, Steven. *A History of the Crusades.* 3 vols. England: Cambridge University Press, 1951.

Stransky, Thomas F. "Crisis of Religion in the Holy Land." *America*, April 27, 1996.

Sumption, Jonathan. *Pilgrimage, An Image of Medieval Religion.* Rowman and Littlefield, 1975.

Wareham, Norman and Jill Gill. *Every Pilgrim's Guide to the Holy Land.* Norwich: Canterbury Press, 1992.

The Way of a Pilgrim. Boston: Shambhala Publications, Random Century House, 1991.

Wild, Robert. *Waiting for the Presence: Spirituality of Pilgrimage to the Holy Land.* Jerusalem: Franciscan Printing Press, 1988.

Wilken, Robert L. *The Land Called Holy: Palestine in Christian History and Thought.* New Haven: Yale University Press, 1992.

Note: Some books are out of print but available in the U.S.A. through the inter-library loan service. Books published in Jerusalem may be available from the Christian Information Center, Jaffa Gate, P.O. Box 14308, Jerusalem, Israel.

Index

Order Information

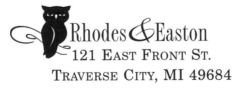

JERUSALEM AND THE HOLY LAND

Cover design by Eric Norton

*Text design by Eric Norton in Adobe™ Galliard
with display lines in Adobe™ Garamond*

Text stock is 60 lb. Windsor Vellum

*Printed and bound by McNaughton & Gunn
Saline, Michigan*

Production Editor: Alex Moore